***This Book Belongs To***

---

YOUR CLUELESS CLONE

YCC

***Welcomes You Champ!***

# Contents

Visit us online at www.neenadayal.com

Original Book Cover by Chisom Ezeh. Modifications by John Layne

Illustrations by John Layne & Neena Dayal

First Edition January 2024.

ISBN for Paperback Version: 978-81-967058-1-7

*I Dedicate This Book*

*To All The Entrepreneurs*

*Who Love*

*The Self-improvement Industry.*

# Acknowledgements

*Bob Proctor, My Mentor. "I Am So Happy And Grateful."*

I am deeply grateful to everyone who made this book a reality.

My mentor, Bob Proctor, for helping me see the light. Your inestimable guidance will stay with me forever.

My friend, Lois Shuart, for suggesting the name *Clueless* in one of our many conversations. And for gladly asking me to start the series. Your love and support are priceless.

My friend, Madhuri Shinde, for giving me the much-needed push that propelled me to write my first book. I am so very grateful to you.

My cartoonist, John Layne, for creating the comics and always putting up with my strenuous schedules. I did some graphics for this book myself, but your help on this book and all my other books is invaluable.

My family, for having unflinching faith in me. Your love makes my world.

And, of course, I am deeply grateful to all the entrepreneurs who love the self-improvement industry and keep enriching it with their wisdom.

# Preface

***"I went to a bookstore and asked the saleswoman, 'Where's the self-help section?' She said if she told me, it would defeat the purpose."***

George Carlin

I have been actively involved with self-help for as long as I can remember.

It made getting through some bad grades in school, which I thought was the end of me, only because a motivational quote came into my twelve-year-old awareness.

Then, someone's bullying and bad behavior may have been a cause enough for me to remain depressed for the rest of my life. And there came an inspiration that struck me and still strikes me after many years. It came from a good book. It said, “This too shall pass.”

Then, in college, a nasty illness made me lose a year. This was enough reason for an academically inclined person like me to just collapse, and give up on everything. But again, help came from some book.

Then, as a grownup, help came from books and other materials many times.

Sometimes, when I was ready to leave everything.

Sometimes, when I was fed up with my relationships, and decided not to get into a relationship ever.

Sometimes, when I was facing a lot of other challenges.

Advice came from family, friends, and other people in my life, from time to time; as I am sure comes to you also - sometimes in overdoses.

I could not take the advice of people whom I believed knew nothing experientially about the problem. I could not share many times with others when I thought that I would get ridiculed or not be taken seriously.

Sometimes, I felt that when the other people were advising me, they were only speaking out of what they may have heard or read somewhere. I rather went to the original materials to get better clarity and make my own interpretations.

Sometimes, I felt that they were only providing some solace and sympathy out of their concern for me. I was extremely appreciative and deeply grateful for their genuinely kind gestures. But, I needed implementable solutions, and they were not available from them.

Some may mock, "Who goes to a self-help book to solve a problem in life?"

Well, "I do!"

And I know for sure that many other people all over the world also do.

The self-help genre has been my "Go-to" for as long as I can remember.

You may have been much more blessed that you never had to seek help outside of your inner circle of people. I think you are very fortunate. But, some of us have a world of loving people around us but no one who could really do the hand-holding we seek.

But one thing was always certain. No materials could help me until I gathered enough courage and strength and decided to help myself. So, self-help is ultimately all about helping your own self. The literature can give a much-needed nudge, push, shove, or boost. But still, the onus of action is upon one's own self.

It works with demand and supply. You feel a need. You seek help from the self-help genre. You find a nugget that strikes at the root of your need. Then your mind starts working without you even knowing about it. Then, something feels fulfilled deep inside of you. You may or may not have found an exact solution to your need, or problem, or challenge. But you find enough strength to grow your own wings to find something that works for you.

This is how life works. The advice can come from any source - people, books, educational materials, and now, audio, videos, and full multimedia repertoire.

As a Consultant and Business Coach, I know I cannot help any individual or organization unless they want to help themselves. No one can. That is why I believe all help is ultimately self-help.

And all improvement grows out of self-help.

It is not just restricted only to the genre of self-help. But it works this way when you want to help your own self and create any kind of improvement in your own life. So, for me, self-help and self-improvement always go hand-in-hand.

**Debate About Terminologies of Self-help and Self-improvement:**

The debate that goes on within the self-help industry about the usage of the terminology of "Self-help" as against "Self-improvement" is something that I find superfluous because:

- Self-help and Self-improvement are both almost simultaneous activities. The former leads to the latter.
- Self-help always begins as an internal mental process, which may happen either on its own or with some external input.
- These external inputs compiled together in the form of literature, educational materials, and multimedia materials have been just collectively called "Self-help."
- Many people like "Self-improvement" as

a terminology better than "Self-help," perhaps as it makes them feel good. "Improvement" is more progressive in connotation than "help."

- In any case, when we look at the Self-help industry, Self-improvement is a predetermined and presupposed outcome.

Self-help has been around for as long as humans have been around. It has been there in the form of advice - sometimes from the elders in the family or community, sometimes from the peer group, sometimes from close friends, and sometimes from complete strangers.

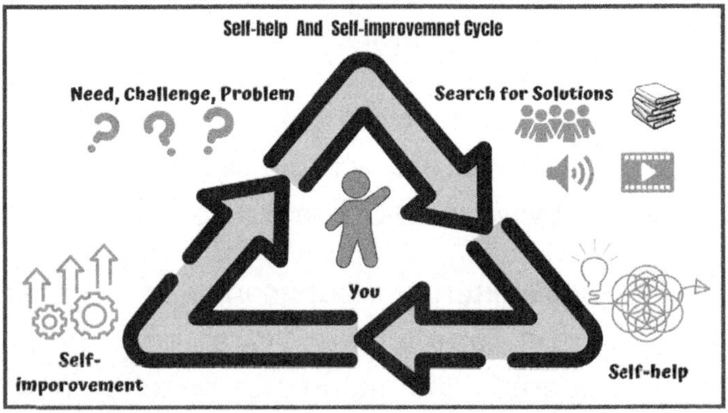


*Self-help and Self-improvement Go Hand-in-hand*

And yet after spending a lifetime with materials, both as a content consumer as well as a content creator, I sometimes feel absolutely *Clueless*. This is because self-help is a journey, and self-improvement is not any single destination. Self-improvement is only a step forward every time it is experienced. This step also gives clarity about the next step, which you must then take.

Being *Clueless* keeps my childlike curiosity aroused for further explorations and further self-improvement.

I find my curiosity leading me to several opportunities. They are equally available to other people also.

The genre of self-help/self-improvement is all about sharing knowledge, observations, opinions, and learnings with tools that are getting technologically advanced. The opportunities for building a business enterprise are immense, both for content creators and content distributors.

Technology is changing so fast that I am a bit *Clueless* about how the whole business will evolve with time. But, I am sure that the segment will grow in leaps and bounds, with new technologies developed to make content creation and content distribution easier and faster.

Do you have generalized or specialized knowledge in any fields and an interest in building a solid business, which you can develop on the side, along with your regular job?

Are you clueless about how to do it?

You are not alone. I, too, was in the same dilemma a few years back. I still feel *Clueless* at times because of the fast-paced growth of technology.

But to start with, this book will give you ample clarity and ideas about how you can participate and build a successful business in the field.

I will be watching the segment of self-help/self-improvement with wide-eyed curiosity and my characteristic *Cluelessness.*

My *Cluelessness* keeps me open-minded about learning, growing, and enriching myself.

If you are interested in this segment, you should watch it, too.

Wishing you all the very best!

***"Always dream and shoot higher than you know you can do. Do not bother just to be better than your contemporaries or predecessors. Try to be better than yourself."***

William Faulkner

*Read On To Know Why I Call Myself "Your Clueless Clone (YCC)?"*

# The Concept of "Your Clueless Clone (YCC)"

## Why Do I Call Myself "Your Clueless Clone (YCC)?"

Hi, my name is Neena Dayal (ND, verbalized as Endee). :-)

As a seasoned Business Coach with a practice spanning many countries, I met diverse people.

I recognized how deeply alike people are despite all their apparent differences.

I also realized how *Clueless* I was, and surprisingly, it wasn't a depressing thought.

My being *Clueless* gives me child-like, wide-eyed curiosity. It thrills me while exploring. It humbles me to be grateful for everything I gain, and for every potential possibility of the future, I have yet to discover.

My *Cluel*essness keeps me from getting stuck-up and hard-nosed...LOL!

As I get to know others, I see that they, too, are *Clueless* about many things despite all their knowledge, expertise, experience, and accomplishments.

In fact, life is a *Clueless* journey. No matter how perfectly you plan everything, the actual steps you finally take on hard ground are always *Clueless.* They always are, and they always will be. That's just how life is designed to be by whoever or whatever created it...Call it Higher Power, Universal Energy, God, or anything else...As you please.

The truth remains static that we all are united in some *Cluelessness*.

So, I am also *'Your Clueless Clone'* (YCC, verbalized as WhyCeeCee) :-)

In every *Clueless* book, you are the Champ!

Together, we go from *Clueless* to Curious to Cognizant.

Welcome to this fascinating and fun-filled journey. **Keep Moving Forward!**

*Transitions from ND to YCC and Vice-versa*

***"Life is Clueless. Keep gathering clues on the forward journey. Maybe, when you reflect back one day it will finally all start making sense."***

# Foreword

**Vikas Saxena**
**Founder & Chief Executive, Professional Expertise Group (PEG),**

**Bengaluru, Karnataka, India**

**Saturday, August 5, 2023**

I am honored and humbled to have been called upon by Ms. Neena Dayal to write the 'Foreword' for her book: 'Clueless About Building A Successful Business In The Self-Improvement Industry.'

I have, during the untrammeled course of our close association which is more than one and half a decade till date, accepted her invite almost always without demur, though, of course after a deliberation between us. But, honestly, this time, my acceptance was instantaneous...yes, it was irresistible and involuntary. In hindsight, I have come to realize, that my acceptance of her invite reflects our strong mutual trust, respect, and confidence.

I have perused the entire text of this book. Notwithstanding the length and breadth of my experience as a professional, spanning over four decades, I attained some height from an intellectual perspective, as Neena's Book is a differentiator in every sense of the term.

Several books in the same genre generally talk a lot about only 'what' to do, but the refrain in Neena's book is not only about 'what' to do but also 'how' to do and how to go about doing it. As if all this is not enough, yet another outstanding feature of her book, which has been consistently addressed and which is palpable, is 'How to build a successful business'... both, aspiring and the accomplished would do well to draw cues from her expositions, marked by zero use of jargons, as jargons can sometimes be liberally used by some writers in the same ilk, and which are unintelligible, blatantly pedantic, and shrill.

Neena has painstakingly, something which is characteristic in her case, punctuated her book with instances relating to situations experienced by various and many in terms of how challenges have been countenanced and how to fix issues. She has cited her own experiences to this effect, and I can testify to both the veracity and her achievements. After all, an example is better than a precept.

Neena Dayal is a highly enterprising and prolific lay professional... a perusal of her book: 'Clueless About Building A Successful Business In The Self-Improvement Industry,' which is unique and non-pareil, will enable one to differentiate the wheat from the chaff.

My sincerest best wishes to Neena!

# Section 1 - Understanding The Self-improvement Industry

***"Every day is a day you can be a better person than you were yesterday. So do something today that your future self will thank you for."***

Oscar Auliq-Ice

Chapter 1

# Why Do We Seek Opinions From Others?

***"People often give us a piece of their mind with the intention to take away our piece of mind."***

Mokokoma Mokhonoana

The entire self-help/self-improvement genre can be seen by some – as people giving their opinions. This is not the correct view because apart from opinionated viewpoints, which do exist, the self-help/self-improvement genre is about multiple and ever-expanding observations, which can be extraordinarily well-researched and authentically effective. Still, the psychology behind giving, taking, and distributing opinions cannot be disregarded while attempting to explore the self-help/self-improvement genre as such.

The path-breaking book by Marshall Goldsmith and Mark Reiter, "What Got You Here, Won't Get You There", takes a perspective that many times we are not able to see clearly how our own behaviors impact our relationships. This is true for both the personal relationships as well as our professional ones.

I tend to endorse this outlook. I have seen this happening in my extensive Business Coaching practice spanning over a decade and reaching out to many countries. I have also seen this happening in my own personal and professional areas.

I have no qualms in admitting at this age and stage in life that I have been as foolish as is possibly possible, in some of my close personal areas. The only saving grace is that, at the same time, I have been extremely astute in my professional areas. So, I know fully well that we can be kind of traveling on two boats at the same time. That's how complicated our relationships can be.

Most of the problems faced by people, and this includes even the top-level executives and entrepreneurs, are due to some kind of breakdown in relationships. The roots of these problems are always in:

**1) Lack of sufficient information of the effective kind.**

**2) Excessive information of the ineffective kind.**

Most of this information is by way of the opinions of others. In the professional areas, very little information is through the official channels. The rest is through the opinions on this official information. That's why grapevine information becomes so crucial to organizations.

The need is to be able to filter all the information brought to us via opinions properly. The need is also not to get too deeply involved in opinions so as to lose track of other, more important things.

I have a friend. I will call him Roy for the sake of saving his real identity. Roy is extremely insecure about himself. We know each other quite well as we belong to the same professional circles. He is good at his work, but some of his habits can get on anyone's nerves.

If Roy comes to know that I have met someone whom both of us know, he makes it a point to ask me, "Did I (meaning Roy) come up in the discussion?" "What did he/she say about me (meaning Roy)?"

It got to a point of annoyance when he started calling me between meetings and during my family time. I came to know through other mutual acquaintances that I am not the only one he pesters.

He is forever calling others, trying to get to know what they have been talking about him behind his back. If he gets praises, he feels elated. If, on the other hand, he gets any kind of a hint of a criticism, he feels annoyed. He can even brood for days and gets depressed.

One day, I met a client for lunch. Both Roy and I had done a lot of work in the past for this client. I deliberately left a message on Roy's voicemail telling him about my lunch plans with the former client. Then, I switched off my cell phone and went ahead with my plans.

Sure enough, as soon as I reached my home office after my lunch with the former client, I saw the light blinking on my answering machine. There were three messages from Roy – each more anxious than the previous one. All his messages implored me to call him and tell him exactly what happened in my meeting...and what the client said about him (meaning Roy).

I did not return his calls.

He called five more times. I let them all go to my voicemail without returning them.

In the morning, he was there in person, standing at my office door, disheveled. I could plainly see that he was furious. I let him in.

We barely exchanged greetings when he launched into how I did not return his calls and how this made him feel. His entire speech was all about himself. I let him release the steam.

Then I asked him calmly, "Were you even concerned about me?" "You know, I never switch off my cell phone, and I always return your calls."

"Did the thought even cross your mind that something could have happened to me?" I calmly said to him.

He just stammered for a moment...then he fell silent...and then he just kept glaring at me. Then he blabbered, "But, I was so concerned about what you were talking about me."

I said, "Exactly! It is always about you in your mind. That's why you think that everyone is talking about you. And that's why the opinions of others matter so much to you."

This may be an extreme example. And, I may have come across as unnecessarily getting involved in a situation, which I could have shrugged off as usual. However, since I was researching for this book at the time, I thought I would see his full reactions if I did not oblige him with all the details of my conversation with the client, as I usually did.

And I saw the extent of his full reactions. He had spent a sleepless, very disturbed night. He sulked. He was angry. He was anxious. He was ready to explode.

The opinions of others matter to us. To some people, they matter so much that they can go to any lengths first to find out the opinions and then to get either elated or get disturbed by them.

Human beings are social creatures. We have taken civilizations, cultures, and societies to the levels they are at today.  For us, connectivity with other fellow human beings matters tremendously. The best way to feel connected with other human beings is through communication.

When people communicate, they also share their opinions. We take opinions from others because it makes us feel connected with them. It is as simple as that.

*Don't Keep Bouncing with Opinions from Others*

## Main Reasons Why We Seek Opinions from Others

- **We like to feel validated.**
- **We like to feel acknowledged.**
- **Both of the above make us feel valued.**

**All of us feel this way, whether we openly agree to this or not.**

What if we receive criticism instead of acclaim when we seek opinions from others?

What if we cannot handle the opinions we receive from others because of their derogatory nature?

What if we get too concerned about the opinions of others?

We need to have enough faith and strength in our own selves not to get swayed by just opinions. And **this is easier said than done.** We all know this.

## Opinions of Others Can Be Productive To Us for Five Important Reasons

**1) We come to know what others really think of us.**

**2) We can take a rational call on what we need to change in ourselves.**

**3) We can take a rational call on which opinions we need to discard.**

**4) We can take a rational call on whom we need to stop paying attention to.**

**5) We can take a rational call on whom to trust with their brutal criticisms as well as honest praises.**

The above are helpful in the progress and growth in both our personal as well as professional spheres.

The emphasis here is on the words "rational call" because if we do not strengthen our internal filters and let ourselves get too affected by the opinions of others, then we can experience a loss in self-esteem. Very serious damages can also happen, which can take us years to recover from.

> ***"Expressing an opinion with an empty soul can complicate your duty of respecting the opinions of others."***
> Vasilios Karpos

## The Counter Reaction

It is quite a trend these days to announce not to consider the opinions of others and to just be yourself and live a carefree life. But since we are social creatures and will always remain social creatures, living this way may not be very effective in the long run.

The entire business model of social media platforms is based on the human tendency to feel connected with other human beings, even if they are total strangers. That's why we see people getting excited on social media over the opinions of others they do not even know or have a chance of ever meeting or getting to know.

Don't get me wrong, please. Social media communication is extremely powerful and a significant step forward in uniting the world in various ways. Disruptive elements who misuse all the opportunities available in today's Internet-empowered world will always be there. Still, no one can deny the power that comes with being able to communicate with someone sitting halfway across the world from you.

Social media has given us the power to express our opinions on anything and everything.

Apart from social media, just being human gives us the privilege to express our opinions.

## Giving Opinions is Important Because...

- It makes us feel significant, which almost everyone loves to feel.
- It makes us feel we are helping others, and

that's a great feeling of being valued.

- It makes us feel the new-found human freedom. Not very long ago, people did not have the freedom to express their opinions. In some parts of the world, they still don't.

- It helps us showcase our knowledge. The knowledge we display to others makes us who we are. It defines our identity. That's why people are known by their professional designations and headlines.

- It makes us develop our self-esteem and self-worth.

- It helps us grow and enrich ourselves. This happens only when we choose to learn from the opinions of others also.

- When we are open to learning, we gain different perspectives from the opinions of other people. This can help us see the errors in our own opinions and change them suitably.

**At the same time, we should never allow the opinions of others to rule our lives.**

**There is a definite way out to maintain the delicate balance, which is mandatory for us to remain approachable – to allow others to express their opinions and for us to remain strong enough to be able to discard the ones that are damaging.**

If giving opinions is important, the flip side is also important – that is, taking opinions in the right manner.

## Taking Opinions from Others is a Critical Exercise

- We can take the sincere opinions of others whom we can trust completely.
- We can use their genuinely concerned opinions to chart our own path to progress and growth.
- We can disregard the opinions of those we cannot trust and keep moving forward on our path to progress.
- Our gut feelings, which are sometimes also called “sixth sense” or “intuition,” are usually the best way for us to recognize our trust in other people.

If we are able to do this, there are strong chances that we can remain productive and efficient even when a sea of precarious opinions surrounds us.

Trust and expectation are absolutely critical in life.

Many people end up saying that you should not have any expectations from anyone. They may even be able to quote scriptures on this. And, if they are good orators, they can actually give a lecture on getting rid of expectations from others. But, they do expect you to listen to them, isn't it? The fact of the matter is that a usual human life cannot be without expectations. We can fare well if we understand expectations properly.

## Major Confusions Happen Because -

- **We make mistakes in deciding whom to trust.**
- **We have higher expectations from people than what they are capable of delivering.**
- **We start repeating both of the above. It sometimes becomes quite a vicious cycle.**

Keeping our eyes firmly glued to the goal up ahead becomes very important in every situation. The goal keeps us focused, and distractions do not happen; or if at all they happen, we can get back on track faster. For this, we need to have a goal. It is immaterial if the goal is small or large. They don't come in any standard sizes. The important thing is that the goal should make us happy and thrilled to remain motivated enough to keep moving forward.

**Keep Moving Forward!** This is the tagline of my company. It keeps me exhilarated and accelerated.

There will always be times when we do feel a bit overwhelmed with all the opinions floating around us. These are the times when we can take a few days' break and just be with our own selves and filter our thoughts, to come back rejuvenated to face the world again.

How other people see us is important for us to know because it helps us change our behaviors accordingly. This can help us gain a lot, both professionally and personally.

***"It is vital to keep an eye on your advisors. People can change, and so are unpredictable. If you keep an eye on them you will know when you should stop trusting them. Your alertness can keep you out of harm's way."***

ND

## Reasons for Taking Refuge in the Books and Educational Materials in the Self-help/Self-improvement Genre

- Many people like the fact that they get unbiased opinions from totally unconnected resources.

The self-help/self-improvement genre is vast and can cover unlimited topics and subjects. Some people like to read and keep themselves updated. They enjoy getting different viewpoints on topics and subjects of their interest. The fact that they can seek opinions on these topics and subjects from totally unconnected and often quite well-established figures is pretty empowering to them.

- Many seek help from books and educational materials in the self-help/self-improvement genre because they sincerely wish to learn, enrich, and grow.

There are certain unconventional study programs that a person can pursue during their leisure time. These can range from hobby courses to leadership programs to complicated computer programming courses. Many people take these and keep enhancing their knowledge during their free time. This has particularly become a trend during the COVID-19 pandemic. So, there is an off-shoot of DIY in the self-help genre.

- Some people resort to books and materials in the self-help/self-improvement genre because they cannot or do not wish to seek help even when facing serious situations.

To such people, I have to say that you get a proper evaluation of your situation. If need be, seek a trusted person whose advice you can respect and let them also evaluate your situation from their point of view. Do not resort only to books and educational materials because they are usually quite generic in nature. It is good if you feel these books and educational materials have been helping you. But, if the serious situation persists and you are unable to handle it, it is always better to seek help from a professional in the field of reference.

- Some people also resort to books and educational materials in the self-help/self-improvement genre because they like to present themselves in a glorious light. They like to quote from trending materials to showcase their knowledge and present themselves better to impress others.

Such people generally have an opinion or know how to formulate an opinion, which they can present with ample third-party endorsement through borrowed materials.

All in all, the books and educational materials from the self-help/self-improvement genre have some observations, research, knowledge, and opinions for everyone.

And this makes them quite an interesting and endearing phenomenon.

*Ouch! Avoid The Opinion Givers When You Read Their Intention of Hurting You.*

***"Opinions are as varied as there are people. Learn to distinguish them well."***

ND

Chapter 2

# What Is The Growth Of The Self-improvement Industry In The Recent Years?

***"The good things about a self-help book is that if you misunderstand something, then it won't mock you."***

Stephen Richards

In the year 2010, I finished studying with Bob Proctor, whom I still consider to be a legend in the Human Potential Enhancement industry. Soon afterward, I started my coaching practice. Since I had an MBA degree and a Diploma in Journalism and Mass Communications, Business Coaching quickly became my forte.

My formal education and past working experience as an advertising executive, plus a flourishing freelance writing business on the side, gave me quite a multifarious cross-cultural experience. I had done some business consulting also, and that gave me quite a few insights into why people do what they do and why they don't do what they know they are supposed to do.

**I realized that no matter what aspirations an organization had unless it attained a proper balance of technology, machinery, and the human component, the growth would not be as desired. As I dug deeper, I kept realizing that behavioral issues were supreme. One could predict all other factors. One could give a statistical analysis about almost everything else in business. One could even predict future growth with quite a bit of accuracy. However, the behavior of the human component was away from any predictions because humans could change their behavior at the drop of a hat.**

I had started creating some human profiles under which the behaviors of people could be slotted. They made me gain some kind of assurance about the way people responded and reacted, but still, the complete solutions were far.

Actually, I had gone to study with Bob Proctor in this kind of predicament. I was quite disgruntled with the human component in my professional areas. And I was facing a terrible time with the people in my close personal areas. The whole idea of human unpredictability was reaching frustrating levels for me. I emerged from Bob Proctor's personal coaching program with a lot of clarity about the human mind and the way people think, act, and interact with other people under different situations and circumstances.

When I started my coaching practice, I created a unique mix of different business topics, plus my new-found knowledge of behavioral issues faced by people. When I focused on all of these different elements, I saw that organizations and individuals started getting results faster and better. This made me see a ray of light, and I started researching these elements more and more.

My full participation as a Business Coach in the Self-improvement industry started by using an online web conferencing product by Citrix Systems Inc. It was called Go-to-Meeting. It was perfect for me as, due to some family situations, I had to move from one city to another quite often. It gave me the liberty to keep developing my coaching practice from the comfort of my cozy little home office. One of my coaching clients, who worked for Oracle at that time, told me about Zoom when it launched in 2011. I used it and found it to be fantastic. It came at a much lesser cost and was much more suitable for my needs to keep my costs low and productivity high.

So, I started out as a Business Coach who worked remotely. It was a new thing in those days when remote working was still a very new concept. It was an exciting new experience, which I enjoyed very much. It gave me the liberty to connect, communicate, and work with people from all over the world. This helped me to establish a worldwide coaching practice. Interacting with people from all over the world strengthened my cross-cultural inclinations and helped me develop wonderful relationships with them. Many of those relationships still continue to this day.

## The Human Potential Enhancement Industry Attracted Me for the Great Opportunities It Offered. The Biggest Benefits I Found were:

- To be able to actually see enhancement in the results of people and organizations I worked with. This mainly happened with their opening up for better adaptability to change and acceptance of growth.

- To experience the immersion of growth and enrichment in my own self.
- Recognition.
- Financial and material perks.
- Humility and Deep Gratitude for all of the above.

**My dream of developing capabilities to actually help organizations see how the people function and help the people realize how the organizations operate was finally getting realized.**

## What Is Self-help/Self-improvement Industry?

Literature in the self-help/self-improvement genre has been around for a few centuries, although the self-help genre got better defined and well-identified only in the last couple of centuries. The self-help genre has now taken the form of a full-blown industry, which is growing at a steady pace. Today, it is a flourishing space with several new writers and content creators and business opportunities emerging almost on a daily basis.

The self-improvement genre started out as being known as the Self-help genre. However, the shift happened because the emotional connotation of self-help was indicative of a sort of helplessness in the users. It showed the consumers as people who were in need of help. This was seen to be counter-productive. Self-improvement, on the other hand, implied the proactive nature of the consumers, who wished for betterment and were ready to take action for this to happen. Another name for this industry, therefore, emerged as the Personal Growth industry.

In this book, I am using both the terminologies - Self-improvement and Self-help. The entire industry is aimed at Personal Growth and Success, so that is obviously the final objective. No one would be interested in Personal Failure, that is also quite obvious. There can be enough personal failure in one's life without any additional help from anywhere. Isn't it?

**In my professional areas, I have always used the terminology - Human Potential Enhancement. I find it more empowering than anything else.**

The consumers of books and educational materials in the self-help/self-improvement genre are eager to learn new skills in order to upgrade themselves and become better versions of themselves.

What is it that makes self-help/self-improvement such an important space? While the reasons can be plentiful and may even differ from person to person, there are certain typical aspects built into the self-help/self-improvement genre, which make it appealing to a lot of users.

In the following points, I give a few details about why self-help/self-improvement space may appeal to different people. This list is not exhaustive, and there can be many more reasons that may be more personal to individuals.

## Books and Educational Materials in the Self-improvement Genre are:

- Content-rich resources that are based on observations, opinions, research, and memoirs of personal efforts.

- Generally, the resources are non-fiction books and educational materials. Some resources are also fiction books. Some of the all-time classic fiction works in the self-help/self-improvement genre are:

"Eat, Pray Love" by Elizabeth Gilbert

"The Alchemist" by Paulo Coelho.

"The Prophet" by Kahlil Gibran.

"The Richest Man in Babylon" by George S. Clason.

"Magnificent Obsession" by Lloyd C. Douglas.

"Tuesdays with Morrie" by Mitch Albom

Many other fiction works can also qualify as shining examples of the self-help/self-improvement genre because they touch a very personal chord that can trigger change in satisfied consumers.

- They usually inspire the readers to accelerate their own efforts to motivate and inspire themselves to achieve their goals and to create an overall improvement in their lives.
- Usually, these books and educational materials are utilized with a self-guided

approach to create enhancement in the intellectual, emotional, financial, and spiritual well-being of the users.

***"I am not a self-help writer. I am a self-problem writer. When people read my books, I provoke some things. I cannot justify my work. I do my work. It's up to them to classify it, to judge."***

Paulo Coelho

- These books and educational materials create an overall enhancement in the self-esteem and self-worth of the users.
- Many times, these books and educational materials encourage users to either create their own support groups or join some existing ones. In these support groups, the users indulge in better utilizing the materials by way of hand-holding with the other participants, who may be struggling with similar issues. They also learn new techniques of empowerment with other participants, who may be striving to achieve similar results in their lives.

- The best thing about the books and materials in the self-help/self-improvement genre is what is said in Stephen Richard's quote at the beginning of this chapter. It is a space that can be utilized totally privately and without any intimidation from anyone.

If you are sitting at the top rung of the corporate ladder, where you are supposed to know all the answers and solve all the problems, it is difficult for you to reach out for help. In that case, you may find solace and help in certain books and educational materials in the self-help/self-improvement genre.

Since the idea of self-improvement is development and growth, the genre covers a wide variety of sub-genres, which are changing with the changing times. This makes the self-improvement industry quite an exciting and dynamic space to watch, learn, and participate in – both as a consumer and as a content creator.

***"Accept only progressive opinions."***

ND

## Statistics of Growth and Future Projections

## Some Facts About The Growth of The Self-Improvement Industry are Interesting As Well As Enticing for Content Creators and Other Business Aspirants:

- The self-improvement industry was estimated at $11.6 billion in 2019. It also took a hit due to the coronavirus pandemic, like all the other industries, and was reduced to be estimated at $10.5 billion in 2020. The market jumped to $11.5 billion in 2021. It is expected to grow steadily at a CAGR of 5% - 6% from 2021 to 2028. The self-improvement industry is estimated to grow to $14.0 billion by 2025. *(Source: Marketdata LLC).*

- According to a report published by NPD, the unit sales of self-improvement books increased at 11% CAGR in only six years from 2013 to 2019 to reach a figure of 18.6 million in 2019. *(Source: Market Research).*

- The number of self-published books in the self-improvement segment even overtook the sales growth. The number of unique ISBNs grew from 30,897 in 2014 to 85,253 in 2019. This indicates the growth in number of new people entering the industry. *(Source: Publishing Perspectives).*

- The interesting fact is that the self-help book market was valued at $800 million in 2018. And the self-help audiobook was valued at $769 million. This shows the adaptability of the consumers to a totally new way of using self-improvement content. *(Source: Market Research).*

- The majority of self-help book authors are men. 62.5% of self-help book readers are women. So, another interesting thing that emerges here is that while more men are writing self-help books, their readership is largely women. *(Source: Quartz).*

- Another area that showed a steep rise was the virtual training, webinars, online coaching, and web-based courses during the lockdown and subsequent work-from-home by almost all organizations worldwide.

- Several holistic institutes also developed their own paid and free online courses.

- Several subgenres emerged in the self-improvement segment. Amongst these, the Health, Gym, Weight Loss, and Fitness Club market was the major one, which is valued at $37 billion. *(Source: IBIS World).* Due to flexible working hours and increased health awareness, people have started preferring to work-out from home instead of taking a gym membership. This has resulted in a significant rise in the demand for fitness equipment. The market, valued at $11.5 billion in 2019, is expected to grow at a CAGR of 3.5% to reach $15.2 billion by 2027. *(Source: Allied Market Research).*

- The top three self-help topics with the consumer percentage are Confidence - 10.2%, Career Guidance, and interview Skills - 7.8%, and Motivation - 7%. The interesting thing is that the percentage of the audience interested in Stress Management is only 0.8%. *(Source: Richard*

*Step).*

- The meditation app market is expected to reach $4.3 billion by 2027. The top ten Meditation Apps earned 195 million in 2019. *(Source: Tech Church).*

- The market for educational toys for the development of the minds of kids is expected to reach $31.62 billion by 2026. *(Source: PR Newswire).*

- Baby boomers have been the steady consumers of self-improvement books and educational materials. Millennials are a close second and are expected to take over soon. *(Source: Market Research).* Some informal projections state that millennials show an interest in investing close to $300 per month on self-improvement books and educational materials. *(Source: BrandMinds).* Women in the age bracket of 40 – 50 years consume more of the self-improvement products and services. *(Source: Brandon Gaille).*

So, all in all, the future looks very bright for the self-improvement industry.

*"And the day came when the risk to remain tight in a bud was more painful than the risk it took to blossom."*

Anaïs Nin

**As a Business Coach, whenever I see future growth projections for an industry, I also see the potential for participation and the prohibitive nature of the competition.**

- The potential of participation in the self-improvement industry is phenomenal for all content creators and other business aspirants.

- With the passing of time, the competition will also keep increasing. But, I always believe that the biggest competition one has is with one's own self. So, the best thing to do is to keep surpassing your own last work.

- Experience matters the most in the self-improvement segment. Age is no bar. In fact, the more you age and the more experience you gain, the better your chances of doing great in this industry. Most of the highly successful Professional Public Speakers and Motivational speakers all over the world are nearing or above 60 years of age.

**So, if you have the grit and creativity to top your own last work, you can always be in demand.**

The strong inclination towards the convenience of digital downloads and virtual learning makes for easy entry into the segment. Today, the market available to anyone is virtually global, with a variety of demographics to target.

The best time to do anything is always NOW. If you have sound knowledge about any topic that can be considered to be included in the self-help/self-improvement segment, have the courage of conviction and take the leap of faith now. The growth of the industry is pretty well defined. What you will do to get a portion of all that moolah is totally up to you.

If you move forward, write to me and let me know your progress. If you feel stuck and need help, reach out, and I will help you move forward.

*You too can have a Soaring Business in the Self-improvement Industry.*

***"The choices you make from this day forward will lead you, step by step, to the future you deserve."***

Chris Murray

Chapter 3

# Why Is The Self-improvement Genre Always Growing?

***"The type of person you are is usually reflected in your business. To improve your business, first, improve yourself."***

Idowu Koyenikan

The self-help/self-improvement genre is definitely not a new emergence. It has been around forever. The authors of ancient Rome and Greece have authored literary works that had a life-changing impact on the audience of their era. They are still considered to be timeless classics.

The greatest of thinkers of all time like Socrates, Cicero, Aristotle, Seneca, Marcus Aurelius, and Plato have all written literature that would qualify as masterpieces in the self-help/self-improvement genre. Meditations by Marcus Aurelius and couplets by Kabirdas, an Indian saint, have been my all-time favorites for their simplicity as well as deep insights.

The most important topic of discussion and coverage in all of the great classics by all of the greatest thinkers was to tell people the way of living an emotionally fulfilling life, with emphasis on moral values, decorum, and decency. They speak about compassion, calmness, humility, forgiveness, leadership, strategic management, war tactics, peace behavior, good parenting, material attachment, money, family values, relationships, feelings, emotions, time management, life engineering, success attainment, failure handling, detachment, religion, awareness, spiritual growth, enlightenment, gratitude, and many more subjects and topics.

This literature has been around for centuries and is still considered to be among the best of the best. This literature is unquestionably under the genres of Self-help/ Self-improvement /Personal Growth /Human Potential Enhancement or any other name you wish to coin for it. And this happened long before the genre actually emerged as we know it today.

Today, self-help/self-improvement is a flourishing industry. Whether we like the trends or not, very few people can deny reading or coming across educational materials that do not fall under this genre. You may not have read a book, but I am sure you must have indulged in reading some articles or blog posts, heard some anecdotes, heard some podcasts, watched some infomercials, seen some television programs, documentary films, or short videos, seen some cartoons and illustrations, or even seen some posters and image posts. These can all be broadly categorized into the self-help/self-improvement genre.

The Self-help / Self-improvement genre has its fingers dipped in every possible medium that you can think of. It has seeped into our consciousness so deeply that even receiving a simple greeting on WhatsApp or any other audio-visual-textual messaging service is not free from it.

And why has something gone so deeply ingrained into our psyches? The reason is very simple - we like it. We like to accept or deny the materials by thinking about them.

When we read a good quote by someone, we feel compelled to think, even if it is only for a brief moment.

The conundrum of our regular lives is so loud at times that just a few stolen moments with something that makes us stop and think a bit can be energizing.

There is a lot of argument both for and against the tremendous growth of the self-help/self-improvement segment into a full-blown industry. But seeing the enormous and continuous growth of the genre, the fact of the matter is still firmly in place that things are not going to change, at least not for quite a while.

**I find it best not to close my eyes to reality. So, I started exploring the reasons for the growth of the self-help/self-improvement genre.**

***"Everything is within your power, and your power is within you."***
Janice Trachtman

## Here's What I Have Found That Makes Self-help/ Self-improvement so Endearing To Us

### Seeking Solace

As the problems of our daily lives become more and more complex, we cannot help desiring and looking for simple solutions. Simple solutions are enchanting because, at the end of a hectic day, we wish for some kind of solace. And what better place to seek it than in an absolutely non-invasive environment of a book, a short video, or an audio telling you some good ways to create a simple life?

### Desire to Make It All Well

Human beings have always liked listening to stories and words of wisdom, where at the end of every turmoil, everything becomes alright. This has been the pet theme of all the bedtime stories we have grown up falling asleep to. Such information is a part of our subconscious mind. Deep inside, we crave everything to become alright...for all our trials and tribulations to end, and we dream of emerging as winners. The self-help/self-improvement genre provides a perfect space where we come across content, the theme of which is that you can remain in control, even when things are going miserably wrong.

## Power of The Mind

I have personally understood the power of the human mind through in-depth study with Bob Proctor, Mary Morrissey, Steve Seibold, and other greats of the world. All humans have access to the mind. Some have developed higher mental faculties to be able to delve deeper into the mind. Good coordination of the brain and mind is needed in order to harness the power of the mind. So, having a perfectly functioning body is perhaps the greatest boon for anyone. However, people facing several challenges with the body can also scale up to access the power of the mind and perform great wonders. To get a better idea about the higher mental faculties, you may like to read my book, **"Clueless About The Differences Between Your Brain And Mind."**

***"Do your best, and be a little better than you are."***

Gordon B. Hinckley

## Simple But Not Easy

After witnessing the full power of the mind, I realized it is very simple. But, it is certainly NOT EASY. So, I, too, am against the books and educational materials in the self-help/self-improvement genre, which make it sound all too easy. It is not. You need a lot of practice and patience to implement the materials into your life.

## Unlearning

Before you can even reach the stage of practice, you need to overcome all that you have learned, all that you have understood, all that is your habit, all that you have witnessed, all that is literally a part of your own fabric, all that is untrue, all that is unproductive, all that has made you fail everywhere in your life.

Unlearning is the most difficult task in the world. It means to overcome your own self. It is like climbing a huge mountain while being completely stripped of all that you can identify with. And this is not even close to enlightenment, as many half-baked books and educational materials suggest.

Getting a mastery over unlearning keeps the mind fresh and far from stagnation. This is what keeps people younger in the body as well.

## The Lure of The Journey

Self-improvement is indeed an awareness-enhancement exercise. But it is a slow and often painful process. If only you are willing to go through all the pain and still continue with the process, you will reach the other end.

After embarking on this journey, I can tell you with full honesty that it is neither easy nor palatable, and it cannot be done only with the help of some books.

Yet, instinctively, humans have always known they have the power and potential to cross all the barriers. How do we know this? Well, I think that the only answer is that we are born with this instinct. This can be called our instinct of self-preservation, although the word "self" needs to be properly and elaborately defined.

The journey lures us, although many times, we may not even be aware of the lure. Humans are creatures who have survived harsh ice ages and still exist all over the globe - right from the equator to the polar regions. We have mastered the different climates and habitats only because we have this immense drive within us that keeps us moving forward. This gives us mental and physical resilience. We are forever dissatisfied with our environments. So, we have to find or create better ones. This means improvement on the existing things. This lure of the journey is woven within us. We just have to do it.

## Unique Mind-Body Interactions

"Self" is not just limited to the physical body. We mostly identify with the physical body because it is the visible structure. We can access it easily with all our physical senses. So, it is the first level of identification that we associate with the "Self."

The mind is a part of our invisible structure. The mind is a movement. It is an activity that everyone indulges in. In fact, our physical senses are the interface through which we interact between the physical structure of the body and the invisible mind.

The mind exists in every cell of our being and even outside of it. We all are floating around in an ocean of activity or movement. This is called the mind.

The primary level of physical interaction happens with the brain. That is why, if in any injury or disease, the brain is damaged, the person cannot establish a connection with the invisible mind, and the person can stay in a state of limbo, sometimes for many years. The mind is still functioning, but the body just cannot interact with the mind. Many coma patients, after waking up and establishing a sufficient mind-body connection, can recall everything that may have happened in the room they were lying in.

Since humans are the highest creatures, our ability to think is the highest. We can think about our external environment as well as we can think about our internal environment. This is a characteristic ability that is not found in other creatures who can think but only with limited potential.

The external environment is outside of us and can be known to others. Our internal environment is known only to us. This is our mental environment, where we think alone. This awareness of our external environment, as well as our internal environment, makes us unique. The ability to think of the external environment as well as to maintain a distinctive internal environment is not found in any other living creature. This is also compounded by the extensive abilities of communication. So, even if animals and plants know about their external and internal environments, they cannot communicate that knowledge with anyone.

We can feel so many different feelings and emotions which are beyond just our instincts. Instincts teach us to survive. Awareness teaches us to desire growth and improvement. That is why all the progress in this world is because of humans. And also the destruction because sometimes we do not know where progress turns destructive. This is also a part of our basic desire to move forward, irrespective of everything else.

***"A dog can be in a room but it doesn't know that it is in a room. You and I can be in a room and we know that we are in the room. This is what makes us so unique."***

Bob Proctor

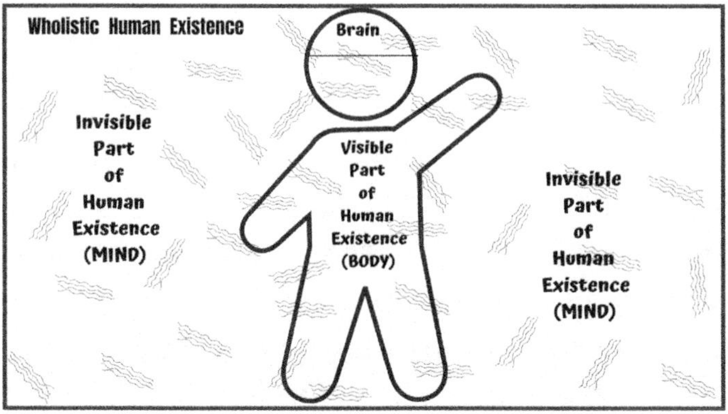


*Wholistic Human Existence has an Invisible Mind Plus a Visible Physical Body*

## Dissatisfaction and Self-improvement

The dissatisfaction we feel is because of our awareness. It propels us to try to improve our situations and circumstances. The problem with this is that most people wish to improve their situations and circumstances, but very few seriously try to create improvement in their own selves.

One argument against the self-help/self-improvement industry is that the genre provides books and educational materials designed to keep people unhappy and dissatisfied. I find this totally baseless because dissatisfaction can increase in anyone due to several reasons. The people who seriously wish to improve themselves find avenues everywhere - in their daily lives. The books and educational materials provide additional assistance. At best, books and educational materials can be treated as additional tools. They cannot substitute for basic desires. Even people who are absolutely illiterate and have never seen any self-help/self-improvement materials can attain massive feats if they truly apply themselves.

I loved watching a critically acclaimed 2015 film called Manjhi - The Mountain Man. This is the true story of Dashrath Manjhi, a simple, illiterate man living in rural India. He was a poor laborer whose wife died in childbirth because he could not reach her to the hospital in time. There was a huge mountain that needed to be climbed to get across to the hospital. There was no road that could take him quickly on the other side.

This man set out to carve a road through the mountain with only the tools that were available to him in his remotely located, extremely poor village. These tools were a hammer and chisel.

**It took him 22 years, but he created a road 30 feet wide and 360 feet long, using only a hammer and a chisel.**

**I am sure this man had never seen any self-help/self-improvement materials.**

If Viacom 18 Motion Pictures and National Film Development Corporation of India (NFDC) had not decided to produce the film, and Ketan Mehta had not decided to direct the film, perhaps we may not even know this story.

It is a story of extreme dissatisfaction and desire for improvement. The only tools needed were a hammer and chisel and a fiery desire to find a solution to the existing problem.

So, dissatisfaction and improvement go hand-in-hand, just as dissatisfaction and giving up do too. The path one takes is solely dependent upon one's own temperament and personality.

Self-help/self-improvement materials only act as tools. They are not mandatory, but they do provide a nice boost and also a cushion to break the impact of the fall if and when it happens.

***"Your inner strength is your outer foundation"***

Allan Rufus

## Timepass Attitude

If someone makes a choice to get addicted to books and educational materials and not take sufficient action, one thing is very clear - the person may not really be looking for any self-improvement.

The self-help/self-improvement genre cannot be blamed for someone's personal choices. This is a bitter pill to swallow.

## Anti Self-help

The anti-self-help genre, which goes contrary to the elements of positive and progressive thinking and basically tells people to remain satisfied with whatever they HAVE, BE, and DO, is also another take on desire and dreams.

It works because of the reverse psychological treatment, along with harsh and even abusive language. It shakes people up to sit up and think and take a closer look at their situations and circumstances. The harsh language adds the fun and realistic element of regular, everyday, ordinary communication, mainly used by youngsters almost everywhere.

## Transmutation of Desire Into Willingness

Till the time the people are dissatisfied with their own lives, the desire to improve their situations and circumstances will remain. The self-help/self-improvement genre should also keep growing.

But desire alone is never sufficient for creating improvements. Unless the desire to grow and improve gets transmuted into the WILLINGNESS to change and fill the lacunae that may exist, nothing happens.

The need is to actually grow the WILLINGNESS to change and create betterment in one's own self. This is purely a personal pursuit. Some people do it, others don't. This is where the human unpredictability factor comes into play.

Again, outside tools from the self-help/self-improvement genre can only provide an additional boost, but they cannot create the willingness. Creating willingness is an internal mental process done purely by the person.

## Growth is a Personal Choice

Sometimes, and for some people, a bad experience in life can accelerate the process of growth. At other times, it can slow down the process, and dejection might set in.

For some people, even a positive experience can accelerate the process of growth. For others, all sorts of material comforts and positive experiences can slow down the process. So, I believe the choice for growth is totally a personal choice. The self-help/self-improvement industry cannot be blamed for anyone making or not making this choice.

> ***"An awake heart is like a sky that pours light."***
>
> Hafiz

## Participation in the Growing Business Opportunity

One reason for the perpetual growth of the self-help/self-improvement genre is the business opportunity that the genre presents.

As far as the opportunity for content creators goes, the self-help/self-improvement industry presents a phenomenal one and will continue to do so. The ones who reap benefits will be those who can present good, workable content in interesting formats for consumption by the users.

Repetitive, stale, and bad content can sell for a while, but it cannot produce long-lasting results with any kind of durability.

There are always good opportunities for entrepreneurs who keep creating new platforms and avenues for content to be displayed upon.

The content that has had perennial value in the self-help/self-improvement genre has always been simple, thought-provoking, non-gimmicky, exertion-oriented, and deeply grounded in reality. The rest of the content just comes and goes like tides in the ocean. What you wish to create is totally up to you.

Opportunities are ample, and there are strong chances that they will always be there and only get better and better evolved with time.

***"There is only one corner of the universe you can be certain of improving, and that's your own self."***

Alduous Huxley

Chapter 4

# Do You Think Self-improvement Books And Educational Materials Create Improvement?

***"No matter how good you get you can always get better, and that's the exciting part."***

Tiger Woods

When I decided to write this book, I wanted to research various aspects of self-improvement literature. I also wanted to take opinions from other people, who I know are both consumers as well as content creators in the genre.

When I posed the question formally and informally to a lot of people, "Do You Think Self-improvement Books & Educational Materials

Create Improvement?" I got such myriad answers that it got all the more interesting.

A few points became very clear to me. All these points are generic in nature because nothing can be said with certainty without a deep research study. At best, these points can be called observations, which are quite close to reality and can be tested and accepted or rejected only with the aid of that rare phenomenon called common sense.

## The Outcome of My Informal Research

### Awareness of the Opportunities

All the content creators are quite aware of the tremendous opportunities the genre provides. Most are confused about how to take full advantage of all of the opportunities. That is why many content creators choose to imitate others. They end up creating content in ways that may be trending at the moment. The trends are always changing. And they discover that they may not be comfortable with the media they may have chosen. Just because some opportunities may have been good for others doesn't mean that they would be good for you as well.

## "I can Do Better Than That" Attitude

When the ones who are still sitting on the side and have not taken a deep dive see the others who are more successful, they invariably have something to say about the content of their more successful counterparts. This 'something' is always in the manner of presentation or the quality of the content itself. They generally think they can churn out better content than their successful counterparts.

Looking at the positive side, I think it is a good thing because it indicates intentions of betterment on the available stuff. Some can also equate such reactions with feelings of jealousy, but that is immaterial because only success speaks for itself. The rest is just speculation.

## Improvement is a Question of Willingness

On the question of improvement, there is a big spoke in the wheel. It always points towards the consumers of the content. Consumers experience improvement only if they exert themselves enough and really...really wish to improve.

So, all my discussions led to the fact that only the WILLINGNESS to improve can create any kind of improvement.

In my observation over a period of more than a decade of working with coaching clients from all over the world, **the WILLINGNESS TO IMPROVE can lead to improvement in the ABILITY TO IMPROVE**. Watch closely. This is not just a clever play of words.

> ***"When confronted with a challenge, the committed heart will serach for a solution. The undecided heart searches for an escape."***
>
> Andy Andrews

## Self-help/Self-improvement Materials are Just Tools

The self-help/self-improvement materials can provide some support, especially when the person cannot reach out to someone for help, either out of their situations, circumstances, or purely out of choice.

I am not suggesting that people should rely on self-help/self-improvement materials and not reach out for help. This is never advisable. But, it is also a fact that many people don't reach out for help, even when they are desperate for help.

## Some People Just Like The Self-help/Self-improvement Materials

Some people read and consume self-help/self-improvement materials because they like to. They find some tips and strategies that may help them, if at all they implement them. Otherwise, they just consume content because they simply like to. Some of these people have developed bedtime reading habits, which solely rest on self-help/self-improvement materials.

There are many highly successful people from various professions who devotedly devour self-help/self-improvement materials.

I have not really seen any highly successful person expressly attributing their success to any particular self-help/self-improvement materials.

Still, the fact that they like to consume content raises another question, "Has the content impacted them subconsciously in any way?" Only a proper deep research study can possibly bring out the real answers here.

We all know the value of repetition of certain concepts, don't we? Repetition of content, which one finds valuable regularly, especially before the conscious mind goes to rest, can have an extremely favorable and forceful impact.

Self-help/self-improvement materials may be helpful only if they are well-researched and well-presented. This is a fact which cannot be refuted.

## Entertainment Value

I want to add one more element here, which is ENTERTAINMENT. Although there may not be many endorsements to this fact but, I still believe that most self-help/self-improvement materials also have an entertainment value. They may not exactly be considered entertaining, at least not in the conventional formats of entertainment. But, if something provides some good feelings, it definitely should be considered having a feel-good factor.

I think self-help/self-improvement materials provide this feel-good factor to consumers. I have myself experienced this good feeling when, after a long and hectic day, I sit down with an energizing book in the self-help/self-improvement genre.

This feel-good factor associated with self-help/self-improvement materials is also undeniably about entertainment, which is away from regular forms of entertainment. It has a calming and rejuvenating effect. Sometimes, that is all you need.

There are some content creators in the self-help/self-improvement genre who think that research means only deep research. They tend to present content that is full of statistical figures and diagrams. This may add some value, and some people may like it too. But, I still feel that content creators should keep in mind that all consumers are not equal. Some may only be seeking some light and entertaining reading and not a research manual.

There is another factor of virtual reading. Reading materials loaded with graphs and charts are hard to follow on electronic devices. The content creators should keep this in mind.

## Nil Preaching

Self-help/self-improvement materials may be helpful only if they do not preach too much. Let us admit it: our teenage children are not the only people in this world who do not like preaching. We ourselves do not like preaching as well.

I have attended some seminars, which could have bored me to death because of the strong preaching elements in the materials as well as presentations.

See, creating improvement or even motivation is actually not about telling someone - "You should do this, and you should not do that." I believe everyone knows what they are supposed to do and what they are not supposed to do. Even a hardened criminal knows deep inside that they are doing wrong things. This is why they ultimately break down after being caught and shown the mirror of reality. I know Criminal Psychology is a much deeper subject, so I am delving into it. I am only targeting you to the next point in this journey of self-improvement.

## Realization is The Cure

Actually, improvement is about exploration and introspection as to why people do not do what they know they are supposed to do. This requires time, effort, and energy to be consistently invested with a strong determination to face all the hits and misses.

My mentor, Bob Proctor, always used to say, "Realization is the cure."

When there is the realization that something needs to be changed, people look for avenues that can help them create those changes. So, the self-help/self-improvement materials should ideally be targeted towards guiding people to realize the change areas. When a change area is identified

Deep introspection should spark the realization of what needs to be changed. This is the key to improvement. If, after introspection, there is no realization for change, then there is certainly a problem that needs to be attended not just by self-help/self-improvement materials but under the guidance of a professional consultant.

## No Short-cuts

Most self-help/self-improvement materials, which are trending today, tend to give short-cut solutions rather than honing the instinctive skills of the people. Instincts are extremely important in order to find solutions for any challenges as well as for learning and progressing.

## One-trick Doesn't Do It All

Self-help/self-improvement materials may be useful only if they do not generalize situations too much. It is true that people have more or less similar problems or challenges in life. But, each one of us is different as an individual. So, the perception of challenges is different for different people, and hence, their handling is also differently done by different people. So, one-trick-does-all actually does not work at all.

There is yet another aspect of results received from self-help/self-improvement materials that I have observed. I would like to explore it under a totally different headline and with another question.

**"Conformity to the present is invisibility to the future."**

Stefan Molyneux

## Do Self-help Materials Breed Falseness?

You may never have thought about the falseness aspect. It is absolutely alright. I, too, started noticing this aspect only a few days back during my research for this book.

See, the rules of demand and supply are highly interlinked. Whenever there is an excessive supply of something in the marketplace, there is always a demand or demand potential for the same, and vice versa. Thus, a surplus supply of self-help materials is also an indication that people may be seriously searching for answers to their growth and improvement challenges, which, in turn, is just wonderful.

The inclination towards falseness in behavior is also quite visible around us these days. Now, I am not saying that it is attributable only to self-help/self-improvement materials. I understand this perfectly. There can be several reasons for the behaviors to become ingrained in falseness. But in my observations and subsequent interpretations, I have come across several situations where, from observing the behavior of people, it is quite evident that they are diligent readers of available self-help materials. This is evident through their conversations, body language, and even parenting styles.

Sometimes, these behaviors may lead to outright manipulations, as seen in the implementation of body language and other communication materials, like in an interview situation, sales calls, or even in some social gatherings. At other times, they verge on total disregard for basic human instincts, especially when it comes to parenting. In all, it is quite an experience to observe such people.

Observing people for their behaviors happens to be my lifelong pursuit and favorite pastime, so it is quite an interesting exercise for me. You can try it too.

**There are some interesting settings in which you can observe people from a distance without becoming noticeable and out-and-out creepy. This is a fun exercise, and you should not risk your own social reputation, safety, and security while doing this. Neither should you put someone else at risk, including the**

**person observed. Remember, while observing others, you, too, get observed by them.**

You do not need any great insights into verbal and non-verbal communication to observe other people. You need to keep your instincts intact and keep yourself grounded in your good intentions and feelings.

Can you spot someone who seems a bit 'unnatural' in his or her communication? Such people seem just a bit overpowering and, well, marginally aberrant. Notice how these people handle their verbal and non-verbal communication if you are within earshot or just their non-verbal communication if you are slightly away.

Another way to spot such people is to look for someone who seems too keen to make an impression. Such people usually act as more informed, suaver, and more 'away from the ordinary.'

You must remember that we are trying to spot unnatural communication traits. Some people are naturally more informed, suaver, and more 'away from the ordinary.' We are not concerned with them here. We are trying to spot those 'actors' who may be trying to 'play' the role of being more informed, suaver, and more 'away from the ordinary.'

When you spot such a person, observe them closely. Very soon, it would be evident to you that they may be trying to manipulate a conversation in the hope of casting a good impression on others by 'appearing' more knowledgeable.

Now, try to befriend this person by striking up a conversation with them. This is relatively easy to do in a social gathering. Do consider your safety and security, as well as theirs, before speaking to total strangers.

See if you can turn the conversation to a known self-help book or even a renowned author of the self-help/self-improvement genre. There are very fair chances that they have been exposed to some such material, if not to the quality material. And there are equally fair chances that they have imbibed the information so readily available these days and, thinking that it gives them an upper edge, are now out to cast 'great' impressions on just about everyone they meet.

## Some Important Directions To Avoid Developing Fakeness while Learning

- There are several genuine learners, and I truly respect them. Through this exercise, we are only trying to spot the fake ones.

- This exercise is difficult to explain logically as it is purely guided by your feelings. But feelings are the surest thing. They never fail to guide you correctly if you have a grip on your intentions.

- Falseness in someone can be due to many factors, mainly insecurities. It may or may not have anything to do with self-help materials. There are no statistics available, but still, I urge you to do this exercise. My observations have led me to many fake learners. Yours may do, too.

- One argument could be that this exercise does not prove that the fault lies with the self-help materials. The fault could very well be with the people who do not do full justice to the information they get. This is absolutely correct.

**Have you ever interacted with a young couple who are also the proud parents of an infant or a toddler? We all can spot such people from our social sphere. Some of us may also dread interaction with them mainly because the whole subject of conversation with them revolves around...Yes...you guessed it right...their babies.**

The example we are citing here is not about the conversation about babies. I do understand people's excitement over their babies. Becoming a parent is absolutely a wonderful feeling. It is about the essence of their conversations. Notice that the main topic of conversation is around how people have difficulty disciplining their children.

Notice how even in regular matters of simply feeding their children three square meals a day, they face immense trouble. In fact, many times, this is the sole point of their conversation. If you have not noticed this so far, I urge you to meet some such people and strike up a conversation about feeding their toddlers. You will soon see what I am hinting at.

Ask someone from the previous generation. Did our parents or grandparents also face such issues with their kids? In all probability, the answer would be a resounding "No."

Think why and when even a simple matter of eating became such a huge focal point.

Think how and when disciplining the children, which was considered a usual way of life, became such an extraordinary effort involving struggle at every juncture.

Evolution is a constant process that is always happening. Presently, evolution is happening mainly at the mental level. This is why the children today are undoubtedly much smarter than the children of yester generations. Now, have the parents also smartened up to become capable of bringing up kids of a smarter fundamental fabric? That requires quite a lot of introspection.

## Here are Some Suggestions To Avoid Falseness In Parenting

Most young parents start reading a lot of parenting literature in the prenatal stages as soon as they come to know about the existence of a child.

Now, there is abundant availability of genuinely great literature on parenting. But most people that I have come across either have not read it or, if they have read it, they have not comprehended it fully, thus failing to implement it in their lives.

For instance, the greatest literature on parenting that I know of comes from the Late Dr. Benjamin Spock. He has given many simple ways of weaning and disciplining babies that are so easily implementable. Above all, as proof, there are generations who have grown into healthy and disciplined individuals upon whom the techniques have been successfully practiced by their parents.

Most other available literature on parenting also gives good tips and can be used wisely if one wishes to.

Yet, why are new parents increasingly finding it difficult to implement the suggestions they have read here and there? The problem arises because of the falseness generated in them. Some of the reading of parenting-related educational materials is read in the hope of appearing suave and aware. It is also done to get an upper edge during conversations.

If, after reading good self-help materials on parenting, you still find parenting difficult and your children are still unruly and difficult to manage, be sure that the problem lies in the implementation of the materials.

Just reading the materials is not enough. Implementation of solutions is absolutely imperative. But if the material transmits feelings of 'know-it-all' and 'fix-it-all,' it may be generating false feelings of superiority in the minds of the parents too, which takes the focus away from finding solutions to challenges and just keeps them happy by feeling 'informed' and 'aware' and even 'appearing smart.'

These are just some simple and common examples that we see everywhere around us.

I am not saying that the behavioral changes that we witness these days are all due to self-help/self-improvement educational materials. What I am saying is that since these materials are found just about everywhere - in the form of books, articles, blog posts, podcasts, videos, image posts, virtual greetings, and GIFs etc, there are heavy chances of anyone coming across them.

See that half-baked information is not imbibed by you in an over-enthusiastic way. Consider this as a bit of a suggestion, that's all.

*The Ever Growing Industry of Self-improvement.*

***"A strong man cannot help a weaker, unless the weaker is willing to be helped, and even then the weak man must become strong of himself; he must, by his own efforts, develop the strength which he admires in another. None but himself can alter his condition."***

James Allen

## Chapter 5

# What Is The Best Tonality In Self-Improvement Books And Educational Materials?

***"We often refuse to accept an idea merely because the tone of voice in which it has been expressed is unsympathetic to us."***

Friedrich Nietzsche

This book is about business opportunities in the self-help/self-improvement industry, so I thought to include a chapter on the tonality used in the books and other educational materials.

There are several different tonalities used in the self-help/self-improvement materials. They are quite interesting to watch. For someone who wishes to create a business for themselves, there is a lot to learn for better synchronization of the materials with their own personalities, as well as with their suitability to their target audiences.

*I begin with a disclaimer. All the examples used in this chapter are for the purpose of illustrating the differentiation created with the variation of tonalities. I have the highest respect for all the examples, tonalities, and content creators who have used them. At any point in this chapter and/or this book, my intention is not to be rude or derogatory to any of the content creators mentioned. All of the content creators mentioned are differentiators and influencers in their chosen topics and areas. They have done a remarkable job of creating impactful content with the tonalities they have perfected. Their voices do not just touch people worldwide, but they also stir them up enough to take notice of their problem areas, find solutions, and produce changes in their own key result areas, which collectively leads to a memorable and outstanding education.*

## Analysis of the Different Types of Tonalities Used by Content Creators in the Self-help/Self-improvement Genre

This analysis is based on my observations. You can use it to craft your own tonality. You can also feel free to add more based on your own observations. I do not wish to suggest that any of these different tonalities are superior or inferior. They are just available for any of the content creators to utilize.

## Preaching Tonality

This is the most common tonality that is seen in various books, educational materials, seminars, podcasts, videos, and other mediums used for self-help/self-improvement materials.

Preaching is about knowing something and then dispensing that knowledge to others in a sermonizing tone of voice. Sometimes, when used in a very heavy voice, this tonality may appear like a superior person lecturing the lesser mortals.

Most self-help/self-improvement literature written with a "You must not do this or that because..." approach falls under this category.

The main thing is that the tone used by the content creators always makes them appear superior to the audience or content consumers. The consumers of this type of content like this tonality. That is why they indulge in it.

As a content creator, you need to be able to carry off this type of tonality. If it suits your personality, by all means, adapt it. You also have to see if your target audience does not get offended by this tonality.

## Teaching Tonality

This is the second most common tonality used in the self-help / self-improvement genre. Most of the content creators who use this approach are trainers. Running the content for the audience is mostly a simple exercise of teaching any preset programs.

The main advantage of this type of content is that more and more people can be trained to duplicate the dispensation of the content.

The materials are written with the approach - "Do this. Don't do that", "How to Do This, and That" and the tonality used can be best described as teaching a class in an emphatic and decisive voice.

Gary Vaynerchuk is a person who uses Teaching Tonality with elan. He also does not come across as a trainer or teacher. At best, he comes across as a person who is knowledgeable and successful trying to help others by dispensing his knowledge.

So, all the tonalities can be modulated according to one's own personality. The comfort level that one brings across with one's personality and tonality is what reaches out and touches another person's heart.

## Friendly Tonality

When I started out in this industry, I found myself to be quite young in comparison with my clients. I was coaching clients who were easily 10 - 15 years my seniors, age-wise. In order to be able to initiate a conversation with them and gain their respect, I had to use a more friendly approach while strategically showing my knowledge by helping them find solutions to their situations.

This worked, and I could establish good relationships with all my clients, with nil exceptions. I also got great references and recommendations, which helped me in establishing my coaching practice.

Since then, I have never used any other tonality. Even now, when I am older than many of my clients or even in similar age brackets as some, I find a friendly tonality works better for me. Once the initial ice-breaking stage is over, I find my clients opening up and sharing more easily with me.

A friendly tonality also works for me because it goes with the natural flow of my basic personality. I can strike up a conversation quite easily with just about anyone, irrespective of the age of the person I am speaking to.

I also intersperse my content with a lot of sensible humor with sensitivity to the users.

In fact, I love speaking with children in the ages of 4 and 5 years upwards because I get to know so much about the way they think about everything around them. Many times, it is just amazing to listen to them and watch them explain things.

A friendly approach and tonality work wonders for me, as it is absolutely effortless for me.

## Experiential Tonality

This is the tonality generally identified with reporting incidents, situations, and experiences. Most of the content found in this tonality is in some specific sub-genre of the self-help/self-improvement main genre. This content can be in the form of travelogues, cooking shows, fitness shows, beauty tips, and others that can qualify for this category.

It is mainly about sharing some experiences that the content creators have themselves been involved in or the experiences they have created for someone else. And during the exercise, or even afterward, they share it with their audiences.

One great YouTube channel where the content is created in Experiential Tonality is from Natasha Ali Lakhani.

## Observational Tonality

Some self-help/self-improvement materials are created in a purely observational style. The present book is in this style.

This style is mainly about observations, analysis, and interpretations. If the materials are presented well, they can be considered to be sufficiently mulled upon. Then, the implementability of the materials may also be considered to be substantiated up to a certain extent.

The whole idea behind the self-help/self-improvement segment is to learn, grow, and enrich. The observations of the content creators thus become a good point of reference to which the consumers are given an opportunity to relate. Many times, the content creators also give consumers an opportunity to add more to their observations. This creates a space for further communication and results in better engagement.

I am also inviting all my readers to contribute more to all of these styles in tonalities that I have mentioned here.

In fact, this book is completely observational. Analysis has been done on the basis of common sense. Interpretations are simple and straightforward. And above all, everything is open to revision and further additions.

## Analytical and Speculative Tonality

In this type of tonality, there is space for lots of graphs, charts, statistics, and analysis. The content creators who use this type of tonality attempt to establish a new hypothesis by analyzing the existing ones.

In this, the content becomes very heavy and research-oriented. This may not be very conducive to be read on electronic gadgets, although this is completely a personal choice. Some people may even be able to read such materials on their electronic gadgets.

Usually, business management, economics, commerce, and financial books are written in this style. And also, lots of multimedia content is created in this way in these subjects.

Most of the business seminars have information backed up by content written in the Analytical and Speculative tonality. This is because the business environment is always changing and is totally dynamic. So, whenever a new thought is presented, it needs to be corroborated with the analysis of a lot of previous information and futuristic speculations.

## Humorous and Mocking Tonality

I see this tonality mainly in the content created by many stand-up comedians. Content creators are also adopting it in the self-help/self-improvement industry. The reason for this is to introduce the element of entertainment in the content of this segment as well.

Humor is interesting to almost everyone. As the self-help/self-improvement industry is adopting the audio-visual medium more and more, the need to generate entertaining content is increasing. That is why Humor and Mocking tonality, which was absolutely unheard of in the previous generations of content creators in the self-help/self-improvement industry, is in the mainstream now.

I see mainly new entrants, who are also quite young, using this tonality. It goes well with the rebelliousness that older people generally associate with the younger generation.

The content generated in this tonality usually has a very high memorability. But the danger of rubbing the audience the wrong way also always looms large.

## Aggressive Tonality

Again, this is something I have mainly seen on the audio-visual medium.

In the Aggressive tonality, there are very tight close-ups used. The speaker may be moving away from the camera and then coming close to it again and again. This repetition causes an aura of not just aggression but kind of a magical feeling. I would recommend watching the YouTube channel of Nick Nimmin to observe this kind of tonality.

Nick speaks in a polite but assertive manner, so Aggressive Tonality should not be confused with aggression in language. I have deciphered the Aggressive Tonality as a specialized style in which the camera is used in a certain deliberate way to create a differentiation for the content creator.

Some people may be using an aggressive tone of voice also. I have seen this, especially on some local YouTube channels. These are mainly in the genre of news reporting, so I have not considered them under the self-help/self-improvement genre.

## Offensive Tonality

The Offensive Tonality is used mostly in what can be best called Anti Self-help Self-help. This has been identified as one of the subgenres of self-help/self-improvement genre. One of the most famous people in this genre is Mark Manson.

The language used is out-and-out offensive, splurged with objectionable words, which are generally not used in decent literature.

The content can expound certain obnoxious areas, which are not really discussed openly. The concept can be totally outrageous, but it is still used for self-help/self-improvement purposes.

A bestselling children's book on Amazon is "The Fart Book" by Mark Bacera. This is a prime example of Offensive Tonality used in self-improvement educational content.

So, this is my categorization of different types of tonalities that I have come across so far in the self-help/self-improvement literature.

I will keep looking for more and add them in the subsequent editions of this book. If the readers come across a tonality that has not been covered here, please do feel free to let me know. I will be happy to add them in the later editions, with deep gratitude and an appropriate acknowledgment to you.

## What is The Best Tonality for You?

**You are the best judge, but here are some criteria to help you make a sound decision:**

- Your own personality.
- Your comfort levels.
- Your target audiences' personalities.
- Your target audiences' comfort levels.
- Your knowledge.
- Your opinions.
- Your experience.
- Your delivery style.
- Your own growth, enrichment, and future objectives.

You can very well use a mix of several different tonalities if that makes you more comfortable and is better suited to the content you wish to create.

There are no hard and fast rules regarding tonality, at least not in the present times. And, as it looks now, this is not going to change in the future as well.

So, do as you please, and go ahead and create the differentiation that makes your content stand out from the rest.

The more differentiated you can make your content, the better your chances of being remembered for a longer duration of time will be. In an age when public memory is getting drastically shortened, and markets are getting flooded with content, the best thing to do is to create memorability with your personal style. And tonality is one of the best tools available for creating your own personal style.

You can read my book, "**Clueless About How To Differentiate Yourself In The Self-improvement Industry.**"

***"Trust is earned, respect is given, and loyalty is demonstrated. Betrayal of any one of those is to lose all three."***
Ziad K. Abdelnour

*Don't Tone Down Your Tone. Play It Up!*

***"Your tone sets the tone."***

Sarah Urist Green

Chapter 6

# How Do Self-help Books And Educational Materials Actually Help?

***"Education does not take place when you learn something you did not know before. Education is your ability to use what you have learned to be better today than you were yesterday."***

Iyanla Vanzant

The bombarding opening line of master psychologist Dr. M. Scott Peck's path-breaking book, 'The Road Less Traveled', boldly announces, "Life is difficult," doubtlessly surmising the essence of life - its difficulties and complications.

Self-help literature is abundant in the markets. Have you ever seen or read any self-help book? Many people may not have read any book as such. But, you pick up any popular magazine or even a newspaper and see columns there that have self-help/self-improvement literature. These newspapers and magazines have a good readership, too. The exposure to self-help/self-improvement literature is exceptionally high, even when people are not really making a conscious decision to indulge in them. Many times, people do not even take any notice that they are reading, listening to, or watching any self-help/self-improvement materials. That is how well-organized the self-help/self-improvement industry has become over time. So, how do self-help/self-improvement materials actually help?

Most people are divided in their opinions when it comes to this question. Some think that self-help materials are really helpful, and others think that it is not so. I feel that both these points of view are quite justified.

***"The whole universe, in its essential nature, is the movement of energy and information."***

Deepak Chopra

**We must remember that the markets are always governed by demand and supply. For any products and services industry to grow to such monumental proportions, there are strong factors that propel it continuously like:**

- Habits of reading or watching or listening to some self-help/self-improvement educational materials.
- A fleeting desire for growth and improvement by the consumers.
- Strong decisions for growth and improvement by the consumers.
- The need for using self-help/self-improvement educational materials as reference materials.
- The desire to take advantage of the self-help/self-improvement industry for entrepreneurial growth.

## How Self-help/Self-improvement Materials Tiptoe Into Our Lives:

### Habit of Materials

Many people who read some sort of self-help material do so just as a form of habit. This is particularly true for people who read self-help materials in newspapers or magazines. They may not even be aware of any real need for improvements in themselves. Hence, they may not even be looking to bring about any improvements in themselves. They just love seeing some new piece every day, or every week, or every month, as the case may be.

### "How To" Solutions Sell

The entire self-help/self-improvement industry has been built on the foundation of consumers seeking solutions to the myriad problems and issues they may be facing.

Therefore, there is a huge market for entrepreneurs who wish to provide self-help/self-improvement educational materials that give “How To...” kind of solutions. Since this material sells, the content creators can definitely help themselves by building good businesses if they take this path.

There can be just about any number of self-help/self-improvement topics that can be made into "How To..." solutions. The present book is also an example of this. The entire *Clueless* series can also be considered as a part of it. It is important to pay attention to the fact that repetitious work does not grab anyone's attention. So, avoid repeating what has been said a million times already, and you can be right on the dot.

## One Size Doesn't Fit All

Many self-help/self-improvement educational materials offer 'one-size-fits-all' solutions, which may not seem feasible and sometimes create exasperation in consumers, but still, they come into the lives of consumers because of solutions they may be seeking about the problems and issues they may be facing.

## Quick-fix is Not Quick After All

The whole essence of life is based on difficulty. Nothing is easy. Right from birth to survival to growth to death, everything that is done for the process of living is difficult. Each one of us has challenges and difficulties in our lives, whether we are born as kings or paupers. But, at the same time, almost everyone has a desire to ease out their lives. This contradiction is a ripe ground for self-help/self-improvement products and services to be sought.

Many self-help/self-improvement educational materials seem to offer quick-fix solutions to challenges. It is quite another debate whether they work or not. But they definitely sell.

## Shortcuts to Growth and Improvement

Life is never easy for any of us. So, how can something as complex as growth and improvement be quick and easy? This fact needs to be considered while trying to expect good results from short-cut solutions. Growth and improvement need continuous exertion. Yet, shortcut solutions make entertaining content that can be enticing to a large chunk of the population. Several social media profiles fall into this category of content, which has high viewership.

## Solutions Come with Honest Introspections

I have seen great value come out of self-help/self-improvement educational materials during my own meditations and introspections. I believe that learning is incomplete unless proper contemplation happens.

If real value needs to be derived from any self-help/self-improvement educational materials, it should include deep pondering. Usually, a lot of suggestions in the materials can be adapted well after proper contemplation and introspection.

## Repetition Works Wonders

One more thing that I have observed is that no self-help/self-improvement educational materials can be grasped in totality the first time. This literature needs to be read and then re-read multiple times in order for you to be able to understand it fully and make it a part of your daily life. This is very necessary to be able to come up with solutions that you may seek for your own situations. Few people may be really doing this.

Repetition is the first law of learning. Watch little kids in kindergartens. Most part of their education consists of repetitions because repetition makes the mind grasp things that may be lost in first reading or listening.

Most people avoid the necessary repetitions and so may not find the necessary solutions from the content they consume.

> ***"How noble and good everyone could be if, every evening before falling asleep, they were to recall to their minds the events of the whole day and consider exactly what has been good and bad. Then without realizing it, you try to improve yourself at the start of each new day."***
>
> Anne Frank

## Insights Follow Exertions

Growth is something that happens in subtle and slow ways. When you go through some self-help/self-improvement educational materials, it is not necessary that you experience growth and improvement immediately. I have seen that many times when I least expect it, an insight comes to me from some materials I may have come across many years ago. This happens during live sessions, seminars, and even when I am creating something.

When you keep flooding your subconscious mind with information, the processing also keeps happening unconsciously. Then, one fine day, the insight jumps at you and surprises you because you were consciously unaware of its existence.

## Personalization Helps

Let us admit it: Unless you make a deliberate effort to go out and purchase any self-help book or any other self-help/self-improvement educational materials and take the advice given therein seriously, you may not see much improvement. And even when you take the advice seriously, unless it appeals to you and touches you in a personalized sort of way, you will fail to implement it to create any long-term results.

Whenever you seek solutions, anything that jumps out and touches you in a personalized way is grasped better, and efforts are made to understand it better. Even if that particular piece of content may have been targeted toward millions of people, few take it to heart because it touches their hearts.

## Referencing Happens

There is another interesting thing that emerged from my informal discussions. Many content creators like to take help from other people's content while creating their own. I am not suggesting plagiarism here. I am speaking of taking inspiration. For instance, if a trainer is preparing content for a training program or seminar, they take help from some books or other self-help/self-improvement educational materials. This is quite a common practice, and I believe credit always needs to be given to the original author or content creator. Doing this gives your audience the impression that you are well-versed in a lot of different materials. It also adds to your humility value, which your audience always prefers to see.

> ***"We must become what we wish to teach."***
>
> Nathaniel Branden

## Enrichment of Conversations

You can use good self-help/self-improvement educational materials to quote in conversations. If this is done not just to create an impression on others, it can add immense value to the conversations.

## Bedtime Stories

One unique way self-help/self-improvement educational materials helped me was to tell bedtime stories to my son while he was growing up. I used to pick up some good anecdotes and stories and then simplify them in a language that my small child could follow easily. I have seen the wonderful value it added to my son's mind while he was growing up. Using self-help/self-improvement materials and converting them into short bedtime stories that can be grasped well by simpler minds escalates the implementable value instantaneously.

***"I will defend the importance of bedtime stories to my last gasp."***

JK Rowling

## Group Discussions

I have also used self-help/self-improvement educational materials to encourage discussions in my group sessions. I have seen people adding great value to the original materials with their own perspectives. Sometimes, the meanings that come out are so highly enriched that they can be implemented much more easily.

Self-help materials are not a quick fix. They can help you only if YOU let them help YOU. So, the center of all self-help/self-improvement activity still remains your own self.

The bottom line is if you like to read any self-help material, it may mean that you have an inner desire to improve and that you are looking to find pathways of self-improvement. But only you can decide what you really want. No book, guide, or counselor in the world can make this decision for you. They can only show you some direction. The ultimate decision to change or not change for the better is always yours.

So consider the self-help/self-improvement books and educational materials as tools that can be used for you to reinvent yourself, and you will find the requisite value in them.

*It May Be Called "Self-help," but it's Always for Helping Others.*

> ***"No matter who you are, no matter what you did, no matter where you've come from, you can always change, become a better version of yourself."***
>
> Madonna

# Section 2 - Understanding The Self-improvement Business Opportunity

***"Do all the good you can while you still have the opportunity."***

Lailah Gifty Akita

Chapter 7

# How Can You Participate In The Self-improvement Industry?

***"If you can get paid for doing what you love, every paycheck is a bonus."***

Oprah Winfrey

The projected growth of the self-help/self-improvement industry is quite well-defined. In order to take a piece of the profit pie, you need to understand how the industry actually works.

Like every other industry, the self-help/self-improvement industry also has some distinctly defined areas where the opportunities for participation never get exhausted. In fact, these areas constantly keep growing and evolving and, therefore, keep offering growth opportunities for all who can upskill and upscale to participate in them.

## Two distinct components of the self-help/self-improvement industry

**Component # 1: The Content or Service Distribution Platforms - Offline Avenues and Online Portals**

**Component # 2: The Content Creators.**

## Essential Elements to be Understood First and Foremost

- Both of these components are important for the self-help/self-improvement industry.
- Both the components always work in conjunction with each other.
- Profitable businesses can be built by utilizing either one of these two components.
- If you wish to participate in this industry, the first step is to decide the component you wish to be a part of.
- You can decide on being a part of one of

the two components.

- You can also decide to be a part of both the components.
- You will need to cultivate separate skill sets for both these components.

***"Keeping busy and making optimism a way of life can restore your faith in yourself."***

Lucille Ball

Now, let's take a closer look at these components of the self-help/self-improvement industry

## Component # 1: The Content or Service Distribution Platforms - Offline Avenues and Online Portals

Since the industry in focus is largely content and services-driven, there must be places where all this content is stored, displayed, distributed, used, and sold for the consumption of the end users.

**Creating and Maintaining These Places, Where All The Content and Services Can Be Hosted, is One Area of Business Activity in The Industry.**

These places can be of the following types:

- **Publishing House**

Books, pamphlets, newspapers, and magazines have been the earliest forms of content dispensation in the self-help/self-improvement industry. They still continue to be an integral part of the whole genre.

You can decide to start your own Publication House if you wish to participate in the industry from this standpoint.

You will need to cultivate an in-depth understanding of the publishing business to avail yourself of all the benefits of this opportunity.

- **Media Production House**

A Media Production House is a place where multi-media production is done. This can be in the form of offline text, websites, audio, videos, full-length films, apps, games, and all other types of media. You can participate in the self-help/self-improvement industry by starting your own Media Production House. If you can develop capabilities in all these areas, it is quite possible to have your own Media Production House. Usually, the best thing to do is to have people around you who are skilled in all the different areas.

The convenience of the virtual environment is such that many people have successfully created profitable YouTube and Vimeo channels where they host multimedia content. **Many of these channels are valued in millions of dollars. So, in a way, these channels act as Media Production Houses without the financial investments needed to start a traditional one.**

Virtual environments have created avenues where the components of the self-help/self-improvement industry kind of overlap each other. Brilliant opportunities emerge from these overlapping areas. All you need to do is think of how to find these opportunities or create new ones and then make the most of them.

- **Educational Web Portal and/or Online Marketplace**

There are several web portals which are knowledge hubs. They work very well as online publishing places. Quora is the best example of this. It is a crowd content company that is expected to reach a valuation of $ 4 Billion in 2022.

There are several websites where content is uploaded and refreshed by the companies who own these websites and not by the inputs from the crowds. In fact, all of the websites have to keep a lot of content in order to get good ratings on search engines so that users can find them easily while searching online.

The content stored thus becomes the currency for web portals and online marketplaces.

## How Websites Make Money

- **Sales of Educational Materials**

This basically forms the online courses segment. Mainly, crowd content is used here. Anyone with specialized knowledge can create their content and host it on these web portals. Usually, uploading the content is free of charge. The web portals make money with a percentage cut on the sale of the content. Examples are Udemy, Teachable, Coursera, and others.

- **Usage Plus Sales of Educational Materials**

The content used here is specialized content created by people specializing in the subjects and topics. These specialists can be in-house employees or freelancers who give their unique content to be sold through the web portals or create exclusive content for them. Examples are Udacity, Outschool, and others. This forms the segment of Ed Tech. Byju's was also a good example, but it has recently declared bankruptcy.

- **Providing a Huge User Base**

The user base is the greatest resource and is interesting to investors for several long-term reasons. The best example of this is again Quora. The content used here is mainly crowd content.

- **Sale of Specialized Gadgets Used Only To Access The Educational Materials**

An example of this is Amazon's Kindle Reading Devices.

- **Advertising Revenues**

Almost all websites make money through the placement of advertisements.

You can participate in the self-help/self-improvement industry by starting any type of web portal and marketplace.

- **Online Educational App**

Almost all of the web portals and online marketplaces also start their own app. This is because virtual behavioral patterns have shown a heavy inclination toward accessing educational materials on mobile gadgets like cell phones, tabs, iPads, etc.

You can participate in the self-help/self-improvement industry by starting a stand-alone educational app.

- **Online Educational Games Marketplace**

Education has become multimedia-oriented because of its great appeal to kids and adults alike. Educational games are a natural offshoot of the multimedia approach because of the extremely high engagement levels they provide. This leads to extremely high learning potential. Examples are Kahoot, Gametize, etc.

There are several educational game portals for the kids. They not just help the kids learn faster and with high levels of engagement, but also help the parents, guardians, and teachers to explain information better. Examples of this are PBS Kids Games, National Geographic Kids, Mr. Nussbaum, Sheppard Software, etc.

You can participate in the self-help/self-improvement industry by starting your own online educational games marketplace.

- **Online Games**

You can participate in the self-help/self-improvement industry by creating your own online educational games. The online games industry is booming because of the very affordable access to the Internet in almost all parts of the world. Examples of this are Eve Echoes, Portal, Free Rice, etc.

- **Video Games**

You can participate in the self-help/self-improvement industry by creating your own educational video games.

In case you are as *Clueless* about gaming as I am, here is the main difference between online games and video games. Online games are to be played while remaining online on mobile devices or computers, while video games are played with video game consoles.

- **Fitness Centers or Gymnasiums**

Fitness is a specialized sub-genre of the self-help/self-improvement industry, which can be content-driven like all other avenues of this industry. The content-driven part forms books, e-books, health websites, online tutorials, podcasts, and others.

Apart from the regular content, you can participate in this sub-genre with the traditional setup of a fitness center or a gymnasium, where health and fitness-related services are provided. Since weight loss and fitness are highly in demand, you can choose to participate in this industry by owning or running your own online portal or an offline fitness center or gym. You can have both as well.

## Component # 2 - The Content Creators:

Since the self-help/self-improvement industry is heavily content-driven, there are always tremendous opportunities available for people who wish to participate in the industry as content creators.

## The Main Opportunities for Content Creation

1. Writing paperback or hardcover books.
2. Writing articles and columns for newspapers, magazines, pamphlets, and other offline publications.
3. Writing e-books.
4. Writing blogs.
5. Writing other web content.
6. Ghostwriting for all of the above.
7. Creating videos on LinkedIn, Facebook, YouTube, Vimeo, TikTok and several other platforms.
8. Creating content as a Professional Public Speaker.
9. Creating content as a Motivational Speaker.

10. Creating full-length educational, documentary, and feature films.
11. Creating podcasts.
12. Conducting webinars.
13. Creating text or multimedia content for apps.
14. Creating text or multimedia content for games.
15. Creating illustrations.
16. Creating individual online courses.
17. Creating specialized online courses.
18. Creating a coaching practice.
19. Combination of a few or all of the above.
20. Freelancing for all of the above.

## Advantages of Starting a Content Creation Business

- You can start your business quickly.
- You can start with very little or even nil

financial investments.

- You can sustain the business single-handedly. Many people start their content creation businesses in their early youth. But age is no bar at all if you have valuable content to share. You can start at any age or stage in your life.

- You can generate great amounts of money in online businesses. Many people have started single-person companies in the last decade. The valuation of many such companies is in millions of dollars.

- You can generate passive income streams very quickly.

- You can create a legitimate and sustainable online business.

You can participate in the self-help/self-improvement industry by creating a business model for yourself that combines both components. This will make your business profitable faster. Of course, you will need to develop separate skill sets for each new area that you wish to attempt, but it is definitely worth the effort.

So, go ahead and do a SWOT analysis right now to get an idea of the right business opportunities for you.

## SWOT Analysis

**The Process I Use for Individual SWOT Analysis is Very Simple. Here it is:**

- Start by taking two simple sheets of plain paper.
- On one sheet, write "Weaknesses" on top.
- Then, start writing your weaknesses point-wise. One weakness should be written at one point. The next one should follow on the next point. This will be easier to read and follow later.
- Make sure that you write in such a way that you use a minimum number of words for each weakness. If you can put your weakness in one word, that is the best thing to do. For example, if you put down "Disloyalty," you do not have to describe it. This list is only for yourself; you know yourself better than anyone else.

- Make sure you remain absolutely truthful on this list. Your future prospects depend upon it.
- Take your time to complete your list. Please do not do this exercise in a hurry. Take a few days if needed. If you are doing the exercise right, you will need several breaks in between to complete the list.
- Do not get discouraged by thinking that you are full of weaknesses. Everyone has their own set of weaknesses.
- Once you are done, you will know it.
- Then, you keep your "List of Weaknesses" aside and start on your strengths.
- Repeat the above steps for your "List of Strengths" also.
- Make sure these are the strengths you really know that you have. This list is only for your eyes.
- Do not write those things on this list that you tell others you have but don't.
- Also, don't write those things on this list

that others tell you that you don't have, but deep within yourself, you know that you have them. For example, others may be telling you that you are lazy. But, if you think you are capable of disciplined hard work and are not lazy, you should put it on the list.

- Be totally honest while making this list. It will affect your future.

- Again, if you are doing this right, you will take time to make this list. Perhaps you may take a few days.

- It is quite common that while making the list of your strengths, you start remembering some weaknesses. If this happens, feel free to pull out your list of weaknesses and make further additions to it.

- Ensure you hide your lists properly so no one else can reach them. This is because this is a deep introspection exercise. While doing this exercise, you are quite vulnerable emotionally. At this time, if someone sees your lists and makes a mockery of them, you may find yourself getting disturbed.

- I also do not recommend writing these lists on your computer or any other electronic device. Use only paper sheets and a pen. This is because writing in traditional ways triggers the thought process in such a manner that facilitates introspection.

- After you are done, take some rest.

- Then, after refreshing yourself, start looking at both your lists. Your Opportunities will emerge from your Strengths. Your Threats will emerge from your Weaknesses. Since you have thought about your Strengths and Weaknesses very sincerely and honestly, these will not be hard for you to see.

- The SWOT analysis done this way is purely for individual purposes and not for organizational purposes. However, I have done this with individuals in organizations in small group settings.

- This introspection exercise makes people see themselves in a new light. This helps them understand themselves better. The first thing to do, which is also highly neglected, is to understand one's own self.

- Most people make career decisions and entrepreneurial decisions based on what others are doing. This does not work in the long run because each one of us has different strengths and weaknesses. Therefore, the threats we feel are unique for each one of us. In the same way, not everyone can take advantage of every opportunity. They are also well suited to us only if they go with the natural flow of the basic fabric of our being.

- There is always a great advantage in accepting ourselves as we really are. This is the first step in moving forward and crossing all obstacles.

- I recommend doing this SWOT analysis every two years. Over a period of time, you will be surprised to see how much you have changed.

- If you are being productive, you will see a trend of your weaknesses either diminishing or transmuting into your strengths. This is indicative of forward movement in life.

- On the other hand, some people see that even their strengths change into weaknesses. This is a sure-shot indication of a lack of progress in life. If you spot such a trend, it is never too late to change it.
- Please remember that life itself is a great opportunity. Whatever you wish to do can be done while you are living. And by the nature of it, life gets shorter with every passing moment. This is not a depressing thought if you are making the most of every moment.

I highly recommend that you do a SWOT Analysis this way once every two years to measure the growth that you experience in your personal and professional areas.

Ideally, you should do a SWOT Analysis every year to check and standardize your growth parameters. But for most people, this may not be a possibility for several reasons. So, you must make it a point to do it once every two years at the least. The SWOT Analysis makes you see your growth or lack of it. It also helps you define your growth parameters by doing the necessary tweaking and adding or deleting the areas as and when necessary based on what you deem important. As you see your growth and improvement, you also realize your future potential, and this keeps you motivated like nothing else does.

*So, What You Choose that Works Best for You?*

***"Because international expansion today happens faster than ever, your company needs a global vision from the earliest possible stage of growth."***

Nataly Kelly

Chapter 8

# How Do You Develop A Profitable Business Model In The Self-improvement Industry?

***"Formal education will make you a living. Self-education will make you a fortune."***

Jim Rohn

Are you interested in developing a profitable business in the self-help/self-improvement industry? If you have read this book to this point, it is a good indication that the answer to this question is a resounding "YES."

## You Must Begin by Understanding a Few Very Important Points

- The "self," in the words self-help/self-improvement industry, starts with you and ends with your consumers - each individual one of them.

- There should always be a direct line of communication established between you and the consumers of your content.
- In the self-help/self-improvement industry, you are the product, and you are also the service.
- The focal point of the business model you create in the self-help/self-improvement industry is, therefore, YOU. The whole business revolves around you.
- The thought that you are the business center in the self-help/self-improvement industry can be both empowering and intimidating, depending upon your own personality.
- If the thought empowers you, you will enjoy being the center of all attention.
- If the thought is intimidating for you, there are pathways in which you can stay behind the scenes and still reap good profits from your business in the

self-help/self-improvement industry.

## For Any Business to Flourish, You Need to Be Clear About Some Power Facts About Money

- **You Wish To Make More Money**

Who wants to make more money? I believe an honest answer to this question would be "YES" - for anyone living in those parts of the world where commerce is a fact of life. This is almost everywhere, except for some remote and still untouched parts of the world.

So, be clear about the fact that you wish to make more money.

- **Interest in Entrepreneurship**

If you are reading this book, chances are you do not just want to make more money, but your entrepreneurial interest is in the self-help/self-improvement industry.

The vehicle of the self-help/self-improvement industry can be an excellent choice for multifarious entrepreneurship interests and involvements.

- **Willingness To Change Your Beliefs About Money**

Some aspects of money are never discussed in polite societies. In fact, a dread of discussing money matters is also introduced in the minds of young kids quite early in their lives. Thankfully, some people in the self-help/self-improvement genre are changing this by writing elaborate literature on money and beliefs connected with money. There are also many online courses available. So, if you need to change your paradigms and belief systems about money, take help from these or reach out for more in-depth help from practitioners in the field of counseling and finance.

I have hired personal financial consultants to take care of all my money matters because, for me, all those calculations are difficult to handle. I just like to keep an overview of all the money that comes into my accounts and remove myself from the intricate and challenging calculations and paperwork.

Many of us have grown up with false and unproductive beliefs about money. Changing them will take you to newer heights hitherto unimagined and unvisioned.

- **Money is Power**

We have to accept the fact that some people have always been more powerful than others. This has been true throughout the history of humans. What makes them more powerful? They are not born with any divine or supernatural powers.

A critical element of power is money, either in personal possession or in one's ability to mobilize it in large amounts. The sooner we accept this fact of human society, the better off we will be in handling our own personal financial matters. Our businesses, jobs, or any other ways we have devised for ourselves to make money are the sources of our power in society.

When we start looking at our jobs or businesses that provide money to us, which is our source of power in society, we start having better harmony with them. We no longer despise our jobs. Or, if we do, we start finding better avenues instead of remaining stuck in a non-functional one. We stop spending our time criticizing our jobs or businesses when we realize that they are our power sources.

- **Fear of Success and Money**

Some people dread money because of the power that comes attached to it. It is a truth that no matter how much we would like to be in power positions, we also fear them the most.

I have spent a lifetime trying to understand people, their mind, their behaviors, and their relationships with success and failure. I have understood a lot about myself in the process. But I can still truly say that whatever I know never feels sufficient. I am still *Clueless* about so many aspects of life and living. Money and the power associated with it is one such aspect.

With great effort, I have been able to clear my mind, up to some extent, of all the wrong information that had been fed into my mind about money. This included the terrible fear of money - both about the scarcity, as well as about the abundance of it. This is a paradox, which I think I will attempt to clear in my future books. I sometimes still feel the dread and tremendous fear gripping me. But now, I identify it quickly and get out of it before it reaches a stage of anxiety. Since I have felt it myself, whenever I see someone going in that direction, I feel a deep urge to stop the person, although, for obvious reasons, I don't act on this urge most of the time. It is mind-boggling for me to see the fear that is there in the minds of perfectly intelligent people regarding money when they are fully aware of the power that money brings along with it.

If we leave the power alone for a moment and consider only the necessity, do you think you can even purchase a cup of coffee or tea if you do not spend the requisite amount of money to cover its price? Being so fearful of something that you need on a daily basis to survive, as well as to thrive, is beyond astonishing to me. And yet, I spent years there, trying to save myself from the clutches of all those advisers who were telling me how my ambition to earn more money might be evil.

- **A Belief that Money is Evil**

One of the biggest fears I have come across is that some people think having money can take away their peace and perhaps make them monstrous and power-hungry. Some even consider money to be dirty or sleazy.

Money is neither dirty nor sleazy. Money is a neutral entity. Money doesn't behave nicely or badly with anyone. PEOPLE DO.

People can be good or bad. Money cannot.

Bad people behave more badly with money because they think they can buy their way out of bad situations by showing power. Good people just remain their good selves, no matter how much money they have.

- **Money Buys Convenience**

Money can buy you a lot of convenience and comfort for yourself and your loved ones. This is the main reason why people want more money.

- **Money is a Standard for Productivity and Achievement**

Money can be a good standard to measure achievement. This is why ambitious people want more money. Ambition is also not a dirty word. Some people look terrible because of their ambition because they fulfill their ambitions by violating the rights of others. Violating the rights of others is never advisable because, in the long run, this can never be productive for anyone. Such people may be able to amass a lot of money, but they eventually lose out on many other areas of life that are equally important or perhaps much more important. One such area is relationships with fellow human beings that can get easily compromised with a blind pursuit for money that involves a violation of the rights of others.

Money is a good standard for measuring your productivity. If you desire to earn more money, it also indicates that you wish to be more productive.

- **Money Ambitions are Good**

If you are ambitious and want to earn more money by using your own knowledge and expertise in creating products or services without violating the rights of others, you need not worry or fear becoming monstrous because of your ambitions.

Only those who do not consider the rights of others and violate them become monstrous.

Again, it is not ambition that makes them monstrous. What they do with their ambition and how they fulfill it makes them what they become.

- Money can help you overcome a lot of problems in your life.

- Money can be given away to help someone else overcome their problems.

- Money can help you in expanding the reach of your services to a far wider audience.

If you are living in the commercial world, money is something you need on a daily basis. And, if you can control your behavior and not turn obnoxious towards other people after you earn a lot of money, it is a perfectly good thing to have.

## Basics of a Good Business Model

I like **Joan Magretta's** definition of the business model. She says, **"A business model is the story that explains how an enterprise works."**

This is an extension to the definition given by **Peter Drucker**, who said, **"A business model answers the questions: Who is your customer? What does the customer value? How do you deliver value at an appropriate cost?"**

I think these are very simple and just phenomenal definitions of a business model. They are also the best ways to create a business model for yourself as an entrepreneur in the self-help/self-improvement industry.

**In the self-help/self-improvement industry, you share your knowledge and tell your story while providing valuable information to your customers at an appropriate cost.**

## For Creating A Good Business Model In The Self-Help/ Self-Improvement Industry, You Need To Realistically Understand The Following:

- **Your own value** in terms of job knowledge, product knowledge, skill levels, and service orientation.
- **Your target markets**. In all probability, different products and services will have different markets.
- **The need** for your products and services to the end users.
- **The value** your products and services create for your end users.
- **The pricing** of your products and services. In all probability, the pricing will also be different for different markets depending upon the paying capacity of the end users.

## Business Strategies

A business strategy is basically a methodology through which a business makes money.

**As Discussed Earlier in Chapter 7, there are Two Distinct Components of the Self-help / Self-improvement Industry.**

## Component # 1: The Content or Service Distribution Platforms - Offline Avenues and Online Portals

## Component # 2: The Content Creators

Both the components of the self-help/self-improvement industry are essential to build a successful and thriving business. They always work in conjunction with each other. One is incomplete without the other. Since both the components are mandatory, there are ample opportunities always available.

There are several strategies commonly used by both the components of this industry. You can choose what works for you. It may be necessary for you to experiment with several strategies to find out the ones that work better for you than the others. A word of caution here – you may see some failure while deciding the right strategies for you. Do not get disheartened with this, and just keep moving forward till you get to the strategies that work for you.

Personally, I like to use a mix-and-match of several strategies. Also, I do not hesitate to choose a different strategy if I find that something is not working. So, flexibility is important, especially when the markets are constantly flooded with emerging competition.

**1) Free Products and Services Strategy**

In this strategy, you keep some or all of your products and services free of any charge to the customers. You earn revenue from the advertisers.

YouTube follows this strategy.

**2) Freemium Strategy**

In this strategy, there are many products and services available for free to the customers who take a basic plan. There are paid upgrades available if you wish to take premium services.

Canva, Thinkific, and LinkedIn follow this business strategy.

**3) Low Upfront Cost Strategy**

In this strategy, the customers pay a low upfront cost for the constant usage of the products or services. There is usually no upper limit of time in this strategy.

Udemy uses this strategy for its course creators. There are several other products like TechSmith Camtasia, Doodly, Toonly, and Infograpia that use this strategy.

**4) Low Subscription Strategy**

In this strategy, there are low costs involved, such as subscription costs to the customers. This is a recurring cost to be paid monthly, quarterly, six-monthly, or annually for the usage of the products and services.

Amazon Prime uses this strategy.

**5) Low-tiered Subscription Strategy**

In this strategy, there is a low-cost subscription available with a tiered approach. Customers can keep getting more services at every tier of upgrade. This is a common strategy used by content creators, who create different courses and educational games.

**6) Percentage of Transaction Strategy**

In this strategy, the revenues are generated as a percentage of the transaction value.

Udemy earns money with this strategy, where a percentage goes to the web portal on every purchase the users make.

**7) Non-revenue Strategy**

In this strategy, the products and services remain always free. The money comes from the investors for providing a large user base. The valuation of the companies keeps increasing exponentially.

Quora and Twitter (Now X) use this strategy.

**8) High Cost of Premium Services**

In this strategy, a high cost is charged upfront for the premium products and services provided. This strategy can be utilized only when there is exceptionally high value attached to your products and services.

I have used this strategy successfully for the last thirteen years in intensive coaching for small groups and individuals.

Other examples of this strategy that I have availed were when I enrolled in Bob Proctor's coaching and Advanced Mind Camp. And also for the Bill Gove Speech Workshop. All of these are premium products. You pay a very high price for them; the value received is phenomenal. So, the interested users, like myself, do not mind paying the high cost.

> ***"The bottom-line is, that nothing should affect your bottom-line."***
>
> Mamur Mustapha

## The Concept of Profit Center

The business models I create are always very simple, sometimes just too simple for the sensibilities of my clients.

People are often interested in complicated figures, past statistics, future projections, and a lot of jargon. While I also take help from all of these, as anyone should, my focus is always on simplicity. This is because simplicity is easy to follow in the long term and can be easily replicated.

For any business to remain profitable, a very simple equation always works -

**PROFITS = REVENUES after subtracting {All Expenses (Even the Smallest Ones) + Working Capital (Whatever is Needed) + 20% of Revenues as Funds Transferred in a Separate Account for Future Growth (Strictly Not to be Touched for Any Other Expenditures) + 10% of Revenues as Funds for Miscellaneous Sudden Expenditures (To Be Transferred Regularly to The Future Growth Fund in Case of Non Usage)}**

Anyone who diligently follows the above equation can build a good business. This is applicable to small businesses as well as to the large ones.

It may not be possible to exactly keep this kind of simplicity in force in larger businesses at a macro level. I believe we can break the larger businesses into several smaller units, where, again, putting this simple equation into practice is quite possible. I also believe it makes the small units into a Profit Center. Having several such small Profit Centers in a large business will always keep the overall business enterprise profitable.

This concept of Profit Centers was first brought to my awareness by a friend and mentor, Mr. Vikas Saxena. He is a consultant running his own consulting enterprise, Professional Expertise Group (PEG), in Bengaluru, India. Since then, I have used it many times with glowing success.

You must consider your own entrepreneurial venture in the self-help/self-improvement industry as a full-fledged enterprise, which you can turn into a Profit Center.

I understand that not all businesses turn into successes. The reasons for failure are not always in the math, science, or art of the business. The major reasons for business failures are in some basic habits that automatically keep manifesting whenever humans come into the picture, which is just about everywhere.

***"Competing on price is what leaves most startup brands bankrupt."***

Bernard Kelvin Clive

## Detailed List of Reasons for Business Failure

**This is Applicable to All Businesses. If You Make Sure to Avoid These, Your Business will Definitely Become a Profit Center and be a Success.**

I use some reverse psychology here because I feel our mind takes notice of negatives faster. That is how almost all of us have been conditioned to think. You must take care of all of these reasons, which look negative and have the capacity to take your business down.

Your business will remain a success in the long term if you take care of these negatives and nip them in the bud. I can almost guarantee your success, provided you do all that is told here.

- **Not Keeping Your Products and Services Always At Top Quality**

Your products and services are most important for your business. They always have to be at top quality. A slight slip in the quality can have long-term adverse effects on the profitability of your business.

- **Not Cultivating Enough Job and Product Knowledge**

This is always a big one, which most people lose sight of, especially after some early success. Always consider yourself, your products, and your services as the best candidates for the highest self-improvement.

Having job and product knowledge is applicable to all businesses and is extremely essential for the self-help/self-improvement business because, by default, your business tells others to improve and grow, so how can you show slackness in having enough job knowledge and product knowledge when your job and products (services) are largely oriented toward growth and improvement?

- **Not Reinventing Your Own Self Continuously**

When you learn, grow, and enrich yourself, you will also keep reinventing yourself.

Integrating knowledge comes with deep introspection and realization of errors and change areas.

Every business needs constant reinventing, remodeling, and revisioning. There are no shortcuts here.

- **Not Creating Enough Differentiation from the Competitors**

One basic requirement of any product or service is to keep differentiating them from those of the competitors. The competition is always tough and massive. The uniqueness that you bring to your products and services is your Unique Selling Points (USPs) and your differentiators. Ideally, your USPs should keep changing for the better with time. Just doing what everyone else is doing is not the path to be taken. This requires deep contemplation and implementation of learning.

Finding out your USPs is perhaps the hardest part of building a business in the self-help/self-improvement industry. Therefore, this is also where most people see failure as they keep looking at the competitors and attempting to imitate them rather than focusing on developing their USPs. The result is that most content creators run the risk of looking like each other's clones rather than appearing to be distinctive.

Creating differentiation also requires a deep knowledge of branding. You must understand that branding is not about just giving a name to your business. Your brand is about what it represents and where it is headed. And this requires a long-term vision and concrete ideologies about your business.

I will publish another book soon on the strategies of differentiation in the self-help/self-improvement industry. So, look out for the book **Clueless About How To Differentiate Yourself in The Self-improvement Industry**.

- **Not Converting Learnings into Knowledge and Skills**

The self-help/self-improvement industry is a process of constant growth and enrichment for content creators. The learnings gained must be constantly converted into knowledge that automatically translates into real-world skills. There can be no compromises on this at any point in time.

The self-help/self-improvement genre is essentially about sharing your message with the intention of creating improvement and growth.

So, the first step is to imbibe enough learnings into your own self.

- **Not Checking the Viability of Your Business Idea**

The viability of your business ideas needs to be tested, and strategies have to be changed with time. Since most businesses are heavily dependent upon technology these days, with the fast-changing technological environment, business ideas also become redundant very fast. So, it is necessary to keep checking the viability of your business ventures. This helps them get a fresh dose of life.

I recently closed down two of my websites because they had to be upgraded to incorporate the changed technological elements, and the business ideas had to be revamped.

- **Not Checking Feasibility of Your Target Markets**

Your target markets also keep shifting. It is a good strategy to start small and then grow to target bigger markets after stabilizing your business.

You can train your target market to get ready to accept your unique ideas if you have patience and vision for your business.

- **Not Understanding the Needs of Your Consumers**

The needs of your consumers also keep changing. They need to be realistically assessed with the passage of time. This essentially means that your message, delivery, products, and services must also keep changing with regularity. Change keeps you alive and thriving in the self-help/self-improvement industry. In fact, change is the only constant in life, and it applies to all businesses.

- **Not Understanding the Direction of Market Movement**

The markets can be in a state of constant flux. It is extremely necessary to assess the market movement properly.

- **Not Controlling Expenditures**

It is important to assess your expenditures from time to time. Most businesses fail because of uncontrolled expenditures.

If you are a content creator, you need to know how to seek out the platforms where you can get maximum exposure at minimum costs.

If you are a creator of platforms, then you need to seek out service providers and employees who can provide good services at reasonable costs. You also need to keep your platforms upgraded to be at par with those of your competitors.

- **Not Pursuing All Available Opportunities and Just Concentrating Egotistically On Only a Few**

This is a phenomenon that is seen happening with regularity. In order to avoid this pitfall, it is necessary that you keep a realistic approach. Sometimes, you may have to chuck out your most loved business idea for unforeseen reasons like unexpected changes in the markets, technology, or political and economic climates of the countries or territories you operate in. Remember, it is important to avoid unnecessary emotional attachments and be pragmatic about your business enterprise.

It is necessary to watch the business situations practically and to explore all available opportunities, even if they do not immediately appear to be an appealing choice. Sometimes, the most unappealing opportunities may turn out to be your greatest assets in the long run. So, keeping a close watch on all the aspects of your business to explore new opportunities or untouched ones is a good idea, and not paying enough attention to this can be a significant reason for failure.

- **Not Enough Networking**

Networking is an important component of all businesses. Meeting and connecting with the right people can boost your business tremendously. Networking is an important way of building relationships. It is a two-way street and needs to be managed with care and concern for the people you are attempting to build relationships with. No one likes to be used. So, do not ever give the impression that you are trying to take advantage of anyone. It does not work in the long run. Networking can be made into a constant endeavor that can be interesting and exciting, not just a dull and drab compulsory activity.

You may like to read my book, **Clueless About Workplace Politics Winning Strategies**. In this book, I have given elaborate details on productive networking.

- **Not Enough Diversification**

Diversification is a necessary part of business growth. Knowing when to diversify is extremely important. Diversification in the self-help/self-improvement business involves different target markets, different target audiences, different approaches, different content avenues, different products and services, and a constantly upgraded mindset.

- **Not Following the Known Best Practices**

There are certain best practices in all the businesses. They are all about the operational and administrative functionalities. They have to be always kept on the right track as a matter of just following the norms. It is not always good to go against the set standard norms. Many people have an undue rebellious attitude, but their rebellion often turns out to be one without a cause because not every rule needs to be broken. Sometimes, the wheels that have already been invented only need to be turned and kept well-oiled.

- **Not Remaining Proactive**

It is important for you to be proactive in your business because it is your business, and perhaps it is most important only for you.

I have seen some entrepreneurs come up with brilliant ideas and then take an ad hoc approach to their business by relying excessively on their employees or outside advisors. This never works in the long run.

It may be an impression that you only need to create an app, a game, or a platform, and then it will keep giving you passive income. This is not the case. For a business to remain sustainable, a lot of work goes in. The most successful entrepreneurs are those who take a deep interest and remain proactive in their businesses. Proactivity also means remaining updated and keeping up with the latest trends. Since the markets are changing rapidly, this is a rather difficult proposition. Therefore, deciding and sticking to your niche is a good idea.

- **Not Conducting Periodic Reviews**

Periodic reviews must be done regularly on all the components of your business.

- **Procrastination on All of the Above**

This is a big one. It appears with constant regularity with everyone. We all are guilty of procrastination. So, just saying that "We must not procrastinate" is never enough. I believe procrastination is a human phenomenon that keeps appearing in our lives every now and then whenever we get too comfortable in our comfort zones. In such times, it is mandatory to remember our goals and objectives, which we wish to attain with our businesses. We get out of our procrastination almost instantly if we are strong enough.

I have attempted to cover all the important points necessary for you to create a profitable business model. I wish you all the best in your entrepreneurial journey. It can be one of the most exhilarating experiences of your life.

If you need further help, you are welcome to contact me for personal consultations.

***"Unfold your today beyond your yesterday, or else, there'll be no tomorrow, only decay."***

Abhijit Naskar

*Technology Empowered Success is Far Easier Than You May Think*

***"The essence of a successful business is really quite simple. It is your ability to offer a product or service that people will pay for at a price sufficiently above your costs, ideally three or four or five times your cost, thereby giving you a profit that enables you to buy and to offer more products and services."***

Brian Tracy

Chapter 9

# What Are Some Of The Lesser-Used Highest-Paying Opportunities For Content Creators?

***"Today the greatest single source of wealth is between your ears."***

Brian Tracy

We live in a truly beautiful world. The Internet has opened avenues that were absolutely unimagined earlier. The opportunities that are available today are phenomenal. They encourage innovation like never before. The Internet is all about content, coding, programming, marketing, and selling. You can make your fortune in any of these areas where your own strengths make you comfortable, knowledgeable, and skillful.

Since this book is all about the self-help/self-improvement industry, I will focus only on the content part here because the industry is largely content-driven. All of the other mentioned activities, like coding, programming, marketing, and selling, are also a part of the background and foreground of the full spectrum of the work that goes on. The ample opportunities for content creators have already been covered in Chapter 7. However, there are certain opportunities in content creation that are less used than the others. They are, incidentally, also the highest-paid ones. So, let us take a deep dive into those as well.

## Three Highly Specialized, Highly Paid Content Creation Opportunities

**(A) Professional Public Speaking.**

**(B) Intensive Coaching.**

**(C) Animated E-learning Programs for Individuals and Organizations.**

***"There are only two types of speakers in the world: the nervous, and the liars."***

Mark Twain

## (A) Professional Public Speaking

I came to know about the extraordinary world of Professional Public Speaking after I came in touch with some of the best Professional Public Speakers in the world, like Bob Proctor, Mary Morrissey, Steve Seibold, Les Brown, Jack Canfield, and others of similar stature.

I had been giving presentations, delivering speeches, anchoring events, and conducting training programs all my professional life. So, addressing large groups of people was not new to me. I used to think that was all what public speaking was about.

Oh! I was so terribly wrong!

Then came a flood of speakers in the markets all over the world who called themselves Motivational Speakers.

A lot of new people started coming into Motivational Speaking sometime around 2007 or so. This was also the time when social media was taking firm roots in human societies all over the world.

The moment someone got out of their notable corporate jobs, the next thing you saw was a change on their LinkedIn profile headline, which now read - Trainer and Motivational Speaker. This was followed by a glowing description of all the in-house training programs they may have conducted, plus all the motivational speeches they may have given.

There came a time when almost everyone who had some kind of generalized or specialized knowledge craved to be in the field of Training and Motivational Speaking.

New YouTube and Vimeo channels started sprouting. New podcasts appeared. New e-books and books were getting published. New follower groups were appearing everywhere in the form of Facebook groups, LinkedIn groups, Triberr Tribes, and on so many other platforms.

In the year 1999 or so, the same thing happened with writing. Web content writing became a very lucrative profession, especially because most of the web content was in the form of articles back then. Almost everyone who knew how to write started aspiring to become a writer.

Web content writing was getting outsourced to countries like India, where English writing is taught at school levels in most of the curriculums. The writers had a unique opportunity to earn in a foreign currency. So, there came a flood of writers and web platforms like Elance, ODesk, Freelancers.com, and many others, which made it possible for content writers to meet their prospective clients. Later, Elance and ODesk merged to become Upwork.

I, too, participated in this and made a very successful business in freelance writing. It is still thriving. I also wrote for newspapers, magazines, and research journals. Since my formal education is in Journalism and Mass Communication and Business Administration, I also started writing for companies for their advertising and media requirements. This led me to start my consulting practice.

I took consulting to the online environment because I just loved the fast nature of communication that happened via the Internet, and the freedom of working from anywhere was the added bonus.

I remember the day I first wrote an email. It was in 1994, and I was consulting with a local export company in India, which had clients in the USA. I wrote the email, and within two minutes, I got a call from the client. It just filled me with a thrill I can still recall after so many years.

I was enamored by the Internet. The power it gave in the hands of common people to be able to communicate instantly with the people sitting halfway across the world from them was amazingly exciting for me.

The final research project for my MBA degree, which I earned in 1997, was on the Effectiveness of Internet Advertising. I remember the tough time I had preparing the thesis for this project, the topic which I had chosen in my overzealousness because there were hardly any research materials available on the topic back then. So, I went out and conducted full-blown research with random sample testing and other paraphernalia. It turned out to be so exciting and enriching.

So, you can see the kind of vision the Internet painted for me.

Although I am a very reserved person, connecting with people comes effortlessly to me. That is why I could build a clientele all over the world with relative ease. This gave me a truly cross-cultural experience, which I have always enjoyed. Many relationships I had developed, even during my freelancing days, are still continuing as beautiful friendships and productive working relationships.

All of this helped me tremendously when I started moving into Business Coaching in 2010.

**And, Public Speaking has been a part of this journey all along. I have seen several aspects of the Public Speaking industry, and after making strong observations, I have developed certain insights.**

> ***"Things do not grow better; they remain as they are. It is we who grow better, by the changes we make in ourselves."***
>
> Swami Vivekananda

There are two distinct segmentations in the Public Speaking industry. These are generally not clear at first glance. So, they need to be understood in-depth.

## The Two Distinct Segments of Public Speaking

### 1) The Troposphere of Public Speaking

The Troposhere of Public Speaking comprises General Public Speaking, Motivational Speaking, and Training Programs.

### 2) The Stratosphere of Public Speaking

The Stratosphere of Public Speaking comprises of Keynote Addresses and Specialized Signature Programs.

**There are Special Characteristics of Both Segments. They can be Elucidated As Follows:**

## 1) The Troposphere of Public Speaking

Refer to Figure 9.1.

### a) Filled To The Brim

The Troposphere of the Public Speaking Atmosphere is filled to the brim with Public

Speakers, Motivational Speakers, and Trainers, and it is getting filled up more and more every day. This is because everyone has realized the worthiness of the profession of Public Speaking, and with the advent of the Internet, everyone has access to a great lot of content.

The charm of Public Speaking lies not just in the display of knowledge but also in the legacy of aura and respect it creates for the speakers. This lures many every day into the profession.

### b) Free Speeches

Several of the troposphere speakers do speeches for free. This is not really a bad thing if you are only trying to break into the field. But I have seen many speakers lowering the price in desperation to get speaking gigs. This not only spoils the market but also lowers the standards and quality of the work done.

### c) First Come, First Served with Success

People who are active in **The Troposphere of Public Speaking** also get paid. In immature markets they may make a lot of money, especially if they have joined earlier.

## d) Needs Heavy Advertising

Sometimes, the ones who can make themselves prominent on social media and advertise a lot in the traditional media can also make themselves a roaring success, even if they join the field later. The audience may be getting more mature with every passing day, but it is the human tendency to look into something that appears several times in front of the eyes. So, advertising still works if done effectively.

## e) No Automatic Graduation

The people in The Troposphere of Public Speaking do not automatically reach the other level, which I like to call **The Stratosphere of Public Speaking**.

The greatest misconception is when people think that if they keep doing good work in The Troposphere of Public Speaking, they automatically get elevated to The Stratosphere of Public Speaking. This almost NEVER happens.

I think anyone who may have been in the field of Public Speaking for some time starts to wonder why they are not getting automatically picked up by the companies. Why is there a constant struggle and tough competition? Why does their caliber not get recognized? Why does ease not come into their Public Speaking business? Why is one forced to constantly compete with the people one knows there is no match in the quality of content, as well as in the style of delivery?

At least, I used to wonder why, despite doing great work and getting good exposure, I was not automatically experiencing the elevation, which, in all humility, I knew I deserved. I realized the answer to this perplexing question after considerable research and contemplation.

This is because the other field, which I like to call - **The Stratosphere of Public Speaking or Professional Public Speaking**, requires a totally different level of training, knowledge, practice, skills, networking, and exposure. It is a different playing field altogether.

## f) Different Levels of Knowledge, Training and Practice

The people in The Troposphere of Public Speaking usually get their training and practice at Toastmasters Clubs. I have great respect for the

Toastmasters Club for the wonderful work they do all over the world.

It is just that I have realized that the curriculum of Toastmasters Clubs can help people do wonderfully well in The Troposphere of Public Speaking. But, The Stratosphere of Public Speaking or Professional Public Speaking, comprising high-paying Keynote Addresses and Specialized Signature Programs, requires totally different training, knowledge, practice, and skill levels.

### g) Immature Markets Behave Differently

Again, in the immature markets, even people from The Troposphere of Public Speaking may get Keynote Speaking gigs. But it is only because the markets are immature, and enough knowledge and expertise still do not exist there. So, the companies do not demand what they know is unavailable in their local markets.

Not every company can afford to get a high-priced Keynote Speaker from abroad who they know will deliver the targeted results they seek.

So, the local people from The Troposphere of Public Speaking keep getting the Keynote gigs. I have seen that many of these people do not even have a remote understanding of what a magical, hair-raising experience a Keynote Address really is.

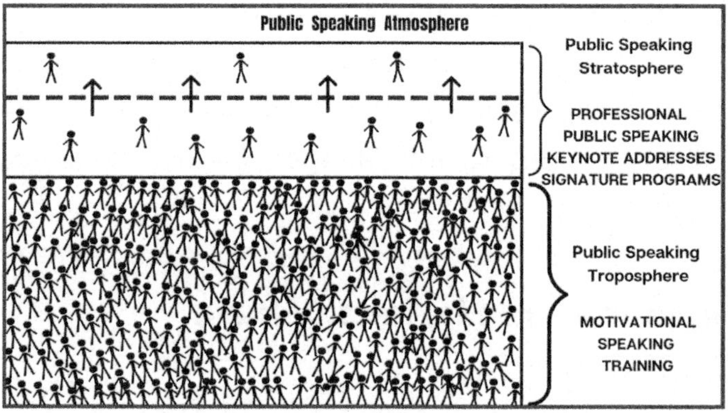


*Figure 9.1: Check Where You Are...Be Honest!*

## h) Enjoy Your Chosen Field of Activity

Motivational Speaking and Training is a different field of activity. If you enjoy doing them, by all means, keep doing them. If The Troposphere of Public Speaking keeps you happy, that is all that is needed. Everyone works for their happiness and satisfaction. But if The Stratosphere of Public Speaking attracts you, know that you will not get there by just doing Motivational Speaking and Training programs.

I do not intend to offend anyone. I am only stating the realities of Public Speaking here, which are hardly ever discussed. If the reality is hurtful to anyone, I can only say to them, "Wake Up and smell the coffee!"

## 2) The Stratosphere of Public Speaking

Refer to Figure 9.1.

### a) Ample Opportunity

The Stratosphere always has ample space and opportunity. There are only a few Professional Public Speakers in it. The situation has always been the same, and it is still the same. And, there is a heavy possibility that it will remain the same in future also.

### b) Space for The Best of The Best

All the **real and best Keynote Speakers in the world** come from The Stratosphere of Public Speaking.

Keynote Speaking is one of the highest-paid activities in Professional Public Speaking. It is an insightful, targeted, and highly specialized area of Professional Public Speaking, which is still the forte of only a few because many don't understand the thorough, meticulous work, extreme effort, deep knowledge, and cutting-edge proficiency that goes into it.

### c) High Payments

On average, a Keynote Speaker from the higher levels in The Stratosphere of Public Speaking gets richer by $20,000 before they even enter the room where they have to deliver their Keynote Address.

The Professional Public Speakers in lower levels of The Stratosphere of Public Speaking also make upwards of $5000 per Keynote Address.

An informal speculation says that there are probably less than 1000 speakers all over the world, who are in the topmost levels of The Stratosphere of Professional Public Speaking. The average net worth of these Professional Public Speakers is upwards of $150 million.

***"No one ever complains about a speech being too short!"***

Ira Hayes

## d) Confusions Prevail in Immature Markets

I see quite a lot of confusion in the markets when it comes to Public Speaking. Even the people who have remained in Public Speaking all of their professional lives may not know about this segmentation. This confusion prevails very highly in immature markets. In the mature markets, where the initial dust has settled, the picture has emerged very clearly, and speakers generally know where they stand.

This segmentation has been done by me purely based on my own observations and learnings. But I remained *Clueless* for a long time. I was also curious for a long time as I knew that there was something that was not getting cleared up.

I had an inkling that it had to be something to do with a different level of activity because, by then, the Internet was giving me exposure to the other level already. So, I finally decided to explore and get down to the bottom of the whole thing.

### e) Witnessing The Hair-raising Experience Clears The Confusion

For me, this confusion finally cleared when I got to see the real action. It is a phenomenal activity that keeps even the C-suite sharks spellbound for those crucial 45-60 minutes when the Keynote Speaker delivers their address. This is because the **Keynote Address is a carefully researched, well-prepared, and thoroughly practiced performance act that keeps everyone sitting on the edge of their seats.**

Imagine why a company would part with that kind of money for a Public Speaking activity, which lasts less than an hour, if they do not get what they are looking for.

When I saw the real action, I was so mesmerized that I became determined to learn this art and science. Then I came to know about **Bill Gove Speech Workshop**, which is the home for the best of the best in the field. So, as a natural progression in my growth journey, I decided to become a part of it. And it has proven to be an extraordinary experience.

## f) Delivering Targeted, Penetrating Solutions

The top-level company executives are always looking for targeted solutions that penetrate through the issues they are facing and can be implemented immediately.

They are not looking for more motivation. Anyone can get plenty of motivation for free on the Internet. They are not looking for preaching in the form of - "You must do this...or you must not do that..." They already know all that and more.

They also know that most of it is only rhetoric and theory, which does not work in the real world.

## g) Celebrity Speakers

The upper echelons of The Stratosphere of Public Speaking also have another slot reserved only for **Celebrity Speakers.** This is a segment where only celebrities who have already made their mark in some other fields can enter. **There is no entry for anyone else.**

The exact price bands for the celebrities are never really disclosed, but we can always speculate that the pricing is based on the stature of the celebrities.

Social media has provided a unique opportunity for almost everyone to reach the stature of celebrity-hood faster. The exposure that social media provides is immense. This visibility can be used carefully to craft one's celebrity stature. This requires careful planning and cultivation, as social media is a double-edged sword that can make or break your reputation and image.

***"There is only one excuse for a speaker's asking the attention of his audience: he must have either truth or entertainment for them."***

Dale Carnegie

## (B) Intensive Coaching

Coaching is another less-used high-paying opportunity in the self-help/self-improvement industry. I say it is less used because coaching can be of many types, and only some types can pay very well.

I started moving towards coaching in 2010, and by 2012, I had a good practice in Business Coaching.

Actually, when I stepped into coaching, my personal situations were such that they did not permit me to work full time unless I took refuge in the Internet. So, I went online and started coaching using a Citrix product called GoToMeeting. Then, when Zoom was launched in 2011, a coaching client of mine who was working in Oracle back then, told me about it. I switched over to Zoom and have loved it ever since.

My personal situations propelled me to go online. And that helped me to build a great business all over the world. I have built a distinguished clientele from all over the world, and I have truly enjoyed the cross-cultural working experience.

I mainly work with mid-to-apex level executives as I love corporate environments. I also work with small business owners because the entrepreneurial spirit just intrigues me as well as exhilarates me.

I have been watching the coaching environment for a long time.

## Some of the Traditional Types of Coaching

### 1) Motivational Coaching

It is all about motivation. Usually, the content here is available in abundance for free.

### 2) Relationship Coaching

As the name suggests, it is all about managing relationships. This can include personal relationships as well as professional ones.

This is a specialized field of activity that needs some base qualifications. Handling the behavior of people is an extremely difficult job. There are no shortcuts here. This is because human beings are the most unpredictable creatures on this planet.

Just having someone boast that they have created good relationships in their lives is not enough for them to qualify as a Relationship Coach.

### 3) Business Coaching

It is about guiding individuals and companies to solve their business issues. The magnitude of the businesses may be start-ups, small businesses, mid-sized businesses, large businesses, and corporate setups.

I love handling all kinds of business matters. More importantly, the roots of my focus are always on people.

You can master the processes, strategies, machinery, and technology rather easily. It is the human factor that is always difficult to handle and keep under check. The human factor also either makes or breaks a business.

### 4) Fitness Coaching

It is all about fitness, weight loss, bodybuilding, healthy diets, healthy living, and other areas of fitness.

Fitness coaching is one of the traditional forms of coaching. It has been around for a long time. Earlier, it was considered to be a part of Sports Coaching because mostly athletes and sports people were using it. Now, fitness has become more mainstream, with generally everyone interested in it. So, Fitness Coaching has also become a very prominent activity.

You can participate in the various sub-genres of Fitness Coaching as a freelancer. Or, you can work as a coach at a Fitness Center. Or, you can have your own Fitness Center. Or, you can join hands with any of the sports teams. These days, almost all tourism activities also have fitness regimes as a value-added service. The possibilities are endless in this field of activity.

## 5) Sports Coaching

All the sports in the world have had Sports Coaches. Without the sports coaches, the players just cannot perform their winning strokes.

I believe Sports Coaching to be one of the oldest forms of coaching activities. Sports Coaching and Fitness Coaching go hand-in-hand.

## 6) Spiritual Coaching

This is quite a popular type of coaching, but these days, it is seen more as a sermonizing activity than actual coaching. There are very few Spiritual Coaches who do the real intensive work in this field of Spiritual Coaching these days.

The *Guru-Shishya Parampara* of India, and several such codes in the oriental region were very popular earlier. They are still existent in some specialized arts. Here the students and their teachers lived in close proximity for many years, in order to learn any art, science, or gain mastery in any practice. It was considered to be the purest form of Spiritual Coaching.

There are some Spiritual Coaches who still practice it in the pure form. For the most part, these days, it has become more of addressing large gatherings of followers, with sermons on spirituality, morals, values, principles, practices, and ethics.

***"Does coaching work? Yes. Good coaches provide a truly important service. They tell you the truth when no one else will."***

Jack Welch

## Some of the Non-traditional Types of Coaching that are Available Today

### 7) Social Media Presence and Marketing Coaching

This is a new type of coaching, which deals with creating a good presence on social media.

Social Media Marketing is a very important activity, which is needed for everyone. So, there is a great demand for this type of coaching.

There is a great opportunity for people who are knowledgeable in different social media. Several people have commanded social media and become Influencers by building good coaching practices. There are several more who specialize in one type of social media and share their insights about that particular social media and have created massive coaching practices.

### 8) Social Media Influencer Coaching

In this, the already existing Social Media Infleuncers share their trade secrets with the others. Such programs fall under what was traditionally known as, Train The Trainer Programs.

How far this knowledge is applicable is something to watch keenly because one question that can come into anyone's mind is - Why would anyone want to share their trade secrets with anyone in such competitive markets?

I believe this knowledge would not be duplicatable. On social media, one's own personality also matters a lot, so everyone may not get similar results.

But, there is a huge demand for these types of coaching programs. And so there is a great business opportunity for people who have knowledge and are skilled in this subject.

## 9) Stress Management Coaching

Stress is a part of everyone's life and is known to be the root cause of most of the health issues. Since demand generates supply, there is a great mushrooming of Stress Management Coaching.

I personally believe this is a part of traditional Relationship Coaching, and is also mandatory in

Business Coaching. So, it is not really a new field of activity.

## 10) Time Management Coaching

This is another type of coaching, which is very prevalent these days. But, it is also a part of all other types of traditional coaching practices.

## 11) Law of Vibration and Law of Attraction Coaching

This is another extremely popular type of coaching activity. I personally believe that it is a part of several traditional types of coaching activities. But many people are doing it as a standalone activity.

I use it as a part of my Business Coaching because the Law of Vibration and Attraction are a part of the Natural Laws of the Universe.

I have been personally mentored by Bob Proctor, and he was the person who brought the Law of Attraction into full public view, when Rhonda Byrne featured him and many others in her book and film, "The Secret."

I am also the only person in the Indian subcontinent to be a part of Bob's Advanced Mind Camp.

I have seen Bob make a topic of Law of Attraction in every program he did. That is how it is supposed to be. It is always a part of a larger activity of understanding the mind and the mental principles, through which you stand in alignment with the Laws of the Universe.

This understanding helps in understanding the behaviors of people, who are part and parcel of all activities that you can possibly imagine.

So, I use this information from the business angle in order to influence the behaviors of people in the businesses I am consulting, coaching, or addressing. I have seen people getting a lot of clarity in what they are doing and why they are doing it when I paint a picture of their mind in front of them. Then, I gently guide them to understand why the Laws of the Universe seem not to support them by showing them that they are not standing in alignment with the flow of The Laws.

Using generalized information about The Law of Vibration and Attraction as a standalone activity does not make much sense to me. But, I am watching people making it a flourishing business opportunity, which again justifies the demand and supply route.

***"The audience will always reflect the energy of the presenter"***

Dr. Lucas D. Shallua

*Does The Law of Attraction Work Everytime? Know When It Does, and How It Doesn't In My Other Books*

## Some Eye-opening Facts About the Coaching Industry

- The litmus test again is, do people wish to listen to you for free, or are they willing to pay you the price you quote? This applies to individuals as well as to companies.

- Please do not think that I am harping unnecessarily on money only. When I started my coaching practice, money was not there in the beginning. It never is for anyone. If you are not innovative and have clarity about your objectives in the coaching business, chances are that money will not be there when you finally decide to quit.
- With so much competition, it is only just and fair that money is earned by those who really deserve it.
- The most clichéd statement you hear from unsuccessful coaches is that they are there to HELP others and do not want to make any money.

Well, it may indeed be true. Chances are that they are not making much money and want you to also NOT THINK of coaching as a viable business when actually coaching is one of the fastest growing businesses in the world.

***"Good coaches truly care about, and help people transform."***

ND

## Some Irrefutable Truths About the Coaching Activity

- Coaching may sound non-inspirational and even irritating sometimes because it is always about honest solutions, no matter how harsh they may sound.

- Coaching is always neutral in approach. A good coach is always non-judgmental. He or she never takes anything as good or bad, no matter what the situation may be.

- Coaching is a gutsy business that does not rest on your being likable to others, even to your clients.

- If you are able to deliver the requisite results to the right kind of clients who are really looking for long-term workable results, you will attain the lasting endearment that all Coaches seek, but only good ones ultimately attain.

- If you are serious about building a coaching business, understand that it is indeed about helping others. And, you can also build a lucrative business if you are really helping them in the right way.

- All Coaches can be Motivational Speakers if they wish to. However, all Motivational Speakers cannot be good Coaches because they may not be able to provide real, implementable, fast-track, and long-lasting solutions.

## Attitudinal Traits of a Good Coach

- Great theoretical & experiential knowledge.
- Phenomenal communication skills.
- Quick thinking, data processing, solid memory, and decision-making with the ability to quickly judge the outcome of proposed actions.
- Hunger to create results with a passion for winning.
- Strong assertiveness without arrogance.
- Ability to be starkly honest and extremely tender at the same time.
- Leadership qualities with penetrating

insights.

- Greatly cultivated intuition.
- Mental Resilience.
- Emotional stability for controlling their own feelings & emotions.
- Ability to remain non-judgmental and impartial while taking a stand, which has a long-term beneficial impact.
- Ability to guide, motivate, and push the clients to take all requisite actions to attain the results they seek.
- Ability to command respect from the clients while forming an open and honest relationship with them.

## (C) Animated E-learning Programs for Individuals and Organizations

This is a highly specialized field of activity, which requires a perfect balance of knowledge, skills, technology, creativity, and the passion you have for Learning and Development (L&D) as a function.

This is also a field of activity that is full of opportunities. There are several companies that provide dedicated services, creating specialized e-learning programs for corporate and educational organizations.

There are some smaller teams that provide e-learning in the form of freelancing services for bigger organizations. And also by creating independent, standalone programs that can be purchased by clients at all levels, ranging from smaller companies to corporate organizations.

I am very fortunate to have created such a team comprising senior L&D professionals. We have created several standalone programs on various areas of business interest.

This is quite an under-utilized area which has great business opportunities. There is ample space for all the talented professionals who wish to make the most of it.

Take the plunge into these lesser-used and very high-paying opportunities for content creation. You will love the rewards they bring into your life.

***"A coach is someone who tells you what you don't want to hear, who has you see what you don't want to see, so you can be who you have always known you could be."***

Tom Landry

*It Takes Incredible Guts To Explore & Succeed In The Lesser Known Opportunity Areas.*

***"You can only become truly accomplished at something you love. Don't make money your goal. Instead, pursue the things you love doing, and then do them so well that people can't take their eyes off you."***

Maya Angelou

## Chapter 10

# Do You Want To Publish Your Book?

***"Find out the reason that commands you to write; see whether it has spread its roots into the very depth of your heart; confess to yourself you would have to die if you were forbidden to write."***

Rainer Maria Rilke

"Oh, how I wish there was someone who could take care of all the extra work that needs to be done in publishing a book and leave me alone with my writing."

I do not know about you, but I wished this so often it almost became my anthem...for not writing my books.

If you, too, are interested in writing and publishing a book but have not been able to understand how the publishing would be taken care of, remember you are not alone to be thinking this way. There are several people who never write a book because of the hassles they think they would be facing while publishing their book.

It is said that everyone has a book inside them. That includes you as well.

That definitely included me.

I have been writing all my life - just not books.

I have been active in all the forms of writing that have been described in Chapter 7 for content creators - just not books.

I had even done a ghostwriting job - writing a book on Personal Wealth Management in the self-help industry - just not for myself.

Then a friend of mine gave me the much-needed push. I will remain eternally grateful to her for this.

And out came a never-ending flood of books, one of which is the present one.

I realized that no matter how high the level of inertia, or fear, or plain laziness is, procrastination never takes anyone forward. Wow! What a realization it was. It's such a simple thing, but sometimes it takes a lifetime to seep through.

The first thing I did was to start writing my first book. Then, as I progressed and completed writing the first section of the book, I started researching for the publishing part also. This is true to my basic nature. When I start doing something, I also start making sure that it reaches its logical conclusion.

I realized that publishing a book has never been easier until the present time. I again thanked my stars for being alive in this time and age when the Internet is so easily available to almost all of us.

The Internet has made available to us so many platforms that have made the publishing pathway absolutely a cakewalk.

***"An author who gives a manager or publisher any rights in his work except those immediately and specifically required for its publication or performance is for business purposes an imbecile."***

GB Shaw

Publishing books is interesting for several reasons. Here are the main benefits of writing and publishing your books and starting your own books publishing business.

## Major Benefits of Writing and Publishing Books

1) Books establish your authority in the subject or topic that you have mastered.

2) Books let your imagination fly and be experienced by others, especially if you write fiction.

3) Books compound your reach to a far wider audience where you may never be able to physically reach.

4) Books survive far beyond your physical life, ans also have a longer shelf life than electronic media.

5) Books let you leave your legacy like nothing else does.

6) Books can earn you passive income and books publishing can be a very lucrative business.

## A Streamlined Outline of All the Publishing Routes Available

### 1) Going Directly to The Publishers

- This is one route, perhaps the most direct and straightforward one. But it works well only for the people who have attained some kind of prominence in any area of activity. It works extremely well for celebrities.

- So, become famous if you wish for this route to work smoothly for you. Becoming famous is not that difficult a task these days owing to social media. Writing is perhaps a much more difficult activity.

### 2) Going Through an Agent

- There was a time, not so long ago, when no good publisher would even touch your book, even with a bargepole, if you did not go through an agent.

- The agents had a nexus with some or all of the leading publishers. The agents did all the fieldwork to get your book submitted to a publisher.

- And then you had to wait for the publisher to make their decision, which would either make or break your writing career.
- The good agents would keep you in business. They would make sure that your books became bestsellers in all the markets they were launched in. and, they got launched in all the possible markets.
- In short, if you landed up with a good agent, you were sorted. You were on the way to becoming a celebrity writer, provided you could also churn out great quality content for your books.
- Getting a good agent is not a very feasible thing, especially in the immature markets. By immature markets, I mean the ones where the pre-publishing industry is not very organized.
- Here is a business opportunity for people knowledgeable in the field of publishing. Having a proper Literary Agency is the need of the hour as there is a sharp increase in the number of people who

wish to write their books. This is especially applicable for the Indian subcontinent, where this segment is not as organized as writers would want it to be.

## 3) Traditional Self-publishing - Paperback or Hardcover Physical Products

Traditional self-publishing is considered to be a bold step because:

- It requires a lot of money investment.
- You have to fight the unspoken questions in the mind of people close to you, who immediately come under a cloud of impression that perhaps your book has not been accepted by any leading publisher.
- It gives you a kind of defiant image, if you approach any leading publisher for the later editions.
- If your book becomes a great success, and you are approached by leading publishers for later editions, then all turns

out well. So, the pathway of traditional self-publishing leaves you with no choice but to write one hell of a book, which gets noticed, picked up, and becomes a roaring success. That is quite a challenge for anyone.

- This publishing route gives limited exposure to your book because of the distribution channels involved that are needed to spread the reach of your book worldwide. So, most books remain localized in exposure. Many self-publishing companies provide marketing support. But, you have to keep investing a lot of money in order to make all the distribution channels function in a well-oiled manner.

***"Some people do not seem to grasp that I still have to sit down in peace and write the books, apparently believing that they pop up like mushrooms without my connivance."***

JK Rowling

## 4) Self-publishing for Independent Authors (Indie Authors): Going Through Publishing Companies – Digital, Paperbacks, and Hardcover Products

- Independent Authors or Indie Authors as they are popularly called, take a route of self-publishing where they retain all the intellectual property rights.

- Indie authors can take a route of getting into a contractual agreement with a self-publishing company or do all the pre and post-publishing tasks on their own.

- Some self-publishing companies have established themselves in every market, which promote indie authors to self-publish while the companies do most of the publishing tasks at a charge.

- The business model of such publishing companies allows them to take the pre and post-publishing tasks off of the hands of the indie authors so that the indie authors are left only with the task of writing and getting their manuscripts ready.

- Some traditional self-publishing companies have started making the books available in digital formats to reach a wider consumer base. For this, they utilize the online self-publishing platforms that are elaborated in the next publishing route.

- If as an indie author you wish to consider self-publishing companies, you should read the contract document carefully because many of the tasks the companies promise to do for you with a considerable charge can be done by you in a much more inexpensive, and perhaps, better way.

- One of the biggest issue in going through this route is that most self-publishing companies make a contract of creating certain number of physical products. The indie authors must invest their money right at the start of their contract, or in some installments before the books get published and launched. This puts pressure on the authors to sell the copies as their money gets locked in and the books get delivered to them. If the books don't sell then this is dead weight that can put considerable pressure on the author and affect their creativity in their future books.

- Realizing the above some of the self-publishing companies don't have the books delivered to the indie authors but they still take upfront costs to cover all the printing and pre and post-publishing tasks for a certain number of print copies. So, the indie author's money still gets locked in.

## 5) Online Self-publishing for Indie Authors: Truly Independent Way - Digital, Paperbacks, and Hardcover Products

- This is the best way to get your books published in the Internet era.
- You can publish your books in the form of digital products plus also physical products like paperback and hardcover books.
- There are several platforms that host e-books, paperbacks, and hardcover books. Most of them allow free uploading

of the books. Some of the platforms ask for a small payment for uploading the books, but still, the amount is minuscule compared to what you end up paying in indie self-publishing. Some of the best-known platforms for publishing books are:

a) Amazon Kindle Direct Publishing (KDP)

b) Ingram Spark

c) Apple iBooks Store

d) Barnes & Noble Press, formerly known as Nook Press

e) KITABOO

f) Lulu

g) Draft2Digital

h) Smashwords

i) Kobo Writing Life

- You can do all the pre-publishing work needed for your books all by yourself.
- You can also hire some freelancers to do the pre-publishing tasks for you. You can

find these freelancers anywhere, maybe right in your neighborhood. They can be college kids who have gained lots of expertise tinkering with their computers. You can hire some local professionals. You can also find them on some freelancing websites.

- The biggest benefit of using online self-publishing is that you can make your books reach all over the world instantaneously.

- This is also an inexpensive way of publishing your books because you don't need to publish your physical products like paperbacks and hardcover books in bulk quantities and then attempt to sell them yourself. Online self-publishing allows you to publish and release your physical books online, and thereafter, they are printed on demand whenever an order is received.

- Physical products like paperbacks and hardcover books are also shipped worldwide to reach a far wider audience than you can reach single-handedly.

Publishing a book has never been easier than with online self-publishing.

***"People can't read a book if they don't know it exists. All authors need to do marketing, regardless of how they published."***

Jo Linsdell

## Marketing Your Books

If you dream of making your book a success, then marketing plays a very important role. You need to properly understand your target markets and then go about creating a marketing strategy to expose your books to your target audience.

Many online courses are available that teach basics and advanced levels of digital marketing. You can try doing those and start marketing your books on your own. However, I believe, some tasks are for specialists. So, if learning all about digital marketing does not entice you enough so you would like to master it the best thing to do is to hire a professional for the marketing of your books because all said and done, marketing is a specialized function that needs to be handled professionally, especially, in such competitive environments.

If you wish to have your books make a good passive income stream for you, it is best to hire some professional digital marketers to do the job.

Again, you may be able to find a good digital marketer in the college kid who lives right next door to you. Or, you can find them online on freelancing platforms.

Now is the time to write your book if you have been waiting to do so.

Find a good thought and avenue and reap the tremendous benefits that come along with it. The greatest benefit is the immense sense of accomplishment and the satisfaction that comes with it.

***"I write from my soul. This is the reason that critics don't hurt me. If I was pretending to be someone else, then this could unbalance my world, but I know who I am."***

Paulo Coelho

*Don't Just Wish! Write Your Book & Publish Online!*

***"As a self-published author, you need to think like an author who writes quality content that people want and need as well as an entrepreneur to establish a marketing system that aggressively markets your books to succeed."***

Bernard Kelvin Clive

# Endnote

***"When you work on something that only has the capacity to make you five dollars, it does not matter how much harder you work – the most you will make is five dollars."***

Idowu Koyenikan

In the end, I just want to add that all the information given in this book is based only on my learnings, observations, experiences, and inferences.

There are no affiliate links anywhere in this book. The products and services I mentioned have either been personally availed by me or I have researched them. And I have found them to be unique and helpful.

I hope that you enjoy reading this book and you find productive information that helps you build a successful business in the self-help/self-improvement industry.

If you wish to tell me about your success as well as your challenges, that you will invariably face, you are welcome to write to me at ycc@neenadayal.com

Enjoy your journey!

All the best!

**Keep Moving Forward!**

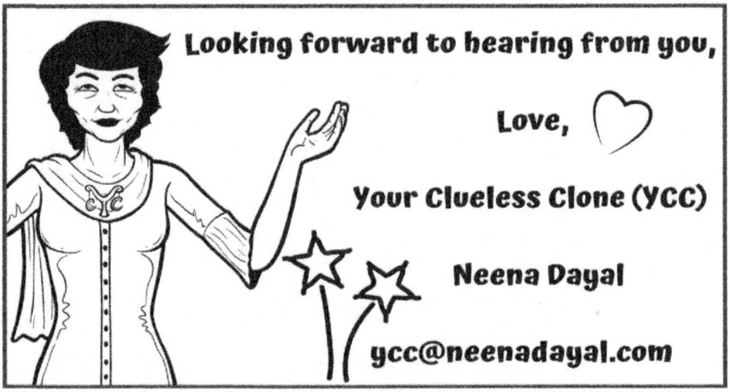


*Come Join The Clueless Club!*

# About The Author

Neena Dayal is a person with multifarious interests and expertise in diverse segments, industries, and verticals. She started out as a Journalist in 1995 and quickly moved to Advertising and Business Consulting before going full-fledged into Business Coaching in 2010.

Neena loves cross-cultural working environments and has been operating worldwide. She connects with people easily, and this makes her behavioral-observational journey productive because people find it comfortable to open up with her.

Her Business Coaching involves humane interactions with a focus on Personal Development leading to business growth.

Her creative expression also finds outlets in paintings, sketches, and doodles.

Neena is intrigued by the mix of myriad human feelings, emotions, and reactions. She studies the human mind and its various manifestations: unpredictability, anger, revenge, jealousy, manipulation, treachery, guilt, subtlety, impudence, courage, bravery, loyalty, and many others under different situations and circumstances. This is her field of research and lifelong study, with which she enriches her Signature Subject, Mental Resilience.

After having a traveling lifestyle for more than three decades, Neena has recently settled down with her family in her native city of Lucknow, UP, India.

# Also By The Author

**Clueless Series** (Please visit: www.neenadayal.com)

1. Clueless About Workplace Politics Winning Strategies.
2. Clueless About Workplace Politics Winning Strategies Work Book.
3. Clueless About How To Build A Successful Business In The Self-improvement Industry.
4. Clueless About How To Differentiate Yourself In The Self-improvement Industry.
5. Clueless About The Differences Between Your Brain And Mind.

6. Clueless About AI Threat To Human Creative Writing.

7. Clueless About Why Persistence Fails? Top Ten Reasons.

**Fiction Books** (Please visit: www.neenad.com)

1. The Avalanche.

2. The Tattoo Man.

3. A Technical Snag.

4. Short Stories for Seniors – Set 1.

## Jot Your Notes

## Jot Your Notes

# Jot Your Notes

Printed in Great Britain
by Amazon

38601255R00136